MASTER TEACHING TECHNIQUES

MASTER TEACHING TECHNIQUES

By
Bernard F. Cleveland, Ph.D.

THE CONNECTING LINK PRESS
387 COOPER'S POND DR.
LAWRENCEVILLE, GA 30244

Fourth Edition, June, 1987

Library of Congress Catalog Card Number:
83-73524

International Standard Book Number:
0-9608678-3-X

Front Jack Design by:

Ward E. Herrmann
Delside Acres Studio
Delhi, N.Y. 13753

The Connecting Link Press
387 Cooper's Pond Dr.
Lawrenceville, GA 30244

Dedicated, with much love, to:

my son, **Bret,**

and to

my daughter, **Anne;**

And to the memory of my father:

Fred B. Cleveland, Sr.

Let us not go over the

old ground

Let us rather prepare for what

is to come.

Cicero

TABLE OF CONTENTS

About This Book viii

SECTION ONE: The Structure of Learning

1	Overview	17
2	Sensory Systems	27
3	Predicate Patterns and Sensory Systems	39
4	Entry Cues	49
5	The Brain	61
6	Summary and New Beginnings	67

SECTION TWO: The Structure of Effective Teaching

7	Overview of Section Two	71
8	The Principles of Learning Revisited	77
9	Establishing Rapport	81
10	Calibration	87
11	Identifying Outcomes	95
12	The Information Gathering Model	105
13	Adding Resources	117
14	The Relevancy Challenge	121
15	The Decision Point	125
16	Remedial Techniques	129
17	Developmental Techniques	155
18	Specific Learning Patterns	170
19	Additional Learning Patterns	176
20	Metaphors	190
21	Submodality Patterns	194
22	Typical Interventions And Their Results	210
23	Choosing An Intervention Technique	216
24	Odds N' Ends	218

APPENDIX 222

ABOUT THE AUTHOR 234

NLP TRAINING 235

GLOSSARY 240

BIBLIOGRAPHY 243

INDEX 244

HOW TO ORDER THIS BOOK 248

ABOUT THIS BOOK

Much of the emphasis in today's education dwells on presenting information, rather than on teaching learners how to learn subject matter. As one of its purposes Master Teaching Techniques fills this void by demonstrating that individuals have "learning patterns" which are well ingrained in their unconscious minds. By developing and modifying these learning patterns teachers can teach children _how_ to learn subject matter! Master Teaching Technique's other purpose is to give you tools which will make you a better teacher! This book contains many practical techniques and interesting information that will aid you in your professional and personal development.

Master Teaching Techniques offers you five major outcomes:

1) learn how to observe and interpret students' non-verbal feedback so that instructional goals can be achieved;

2) learn powerful rapport-building techniques;

3) learn techniques that will assist students in developing alternative responses in situations where such options are needed;

4) learn how to elicit and to install learning patterns;

5) make the teaching-learning process more productive and enjoyable for both teachers and students!

Neuro-Linguistic Programming, (NLP), is a fascinating new field that combines the study of non-verbal feedback and language patterns to improve communication and to bring about rapid behavioral change. In the early 1970's, Richard Bandler and John Grinder, modeled master teachers and influencers, and therapists who could bring about rapid behavioral changes in their clients. The model they developed teaches people to use non-verbal feedback and verbal cues to develop superior comunication methods: how to establish rapport, gather information and to detect and match a person's preferred method of communication. In addition, it teaches a number of powerful techniques that are designed to bring about rapid and benefical interpersonal changes. One of the things that makes NLP so exciting, is that the model is continually evolving. NLP has proven to be an important aid to such diverse fields as education, athletics, sales and management.

Master Teaching Techniques assists teachers in organizing and presenting classroom subject matter in such a manner that successful communication and superior teaching become the norm, rather than an occasional achievement. It also shows teachers how to become "behavioral engineers" so they can assist students in learning more easily.

Successful Teaching

Experienced teachers already know successful teaching requires expertise in diverse areas ranging from developing a classroom physical environment that has a positive effect on the learning process, to knowledge of subject matter and knowledge of the psychology of learning. An example of a superior physical classroom environment includes many of these qualities.

Fig. I: <u>The Ideal Physical Classroom Environment</u>

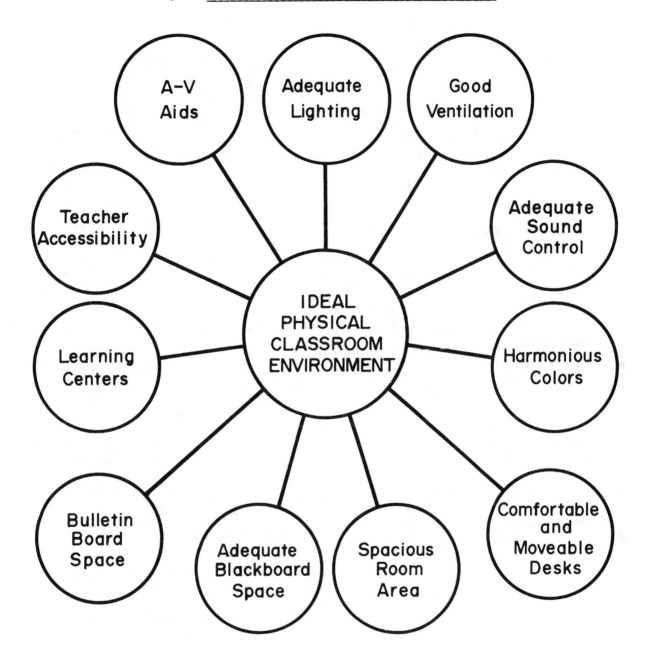

These ideas are self-explanatory and can serve as a comparison check for you. Perhaps they will encourage and stimulate you to improve the physical part of your classroom environment.

Continual research in the last ten years has greatly expanded our knowledge of the learning process. Learning is much more of a complex skill than educators once believed. The following diagram touches on most of the significant factors affecting the learning process.

Fig. 2: The Learning Process

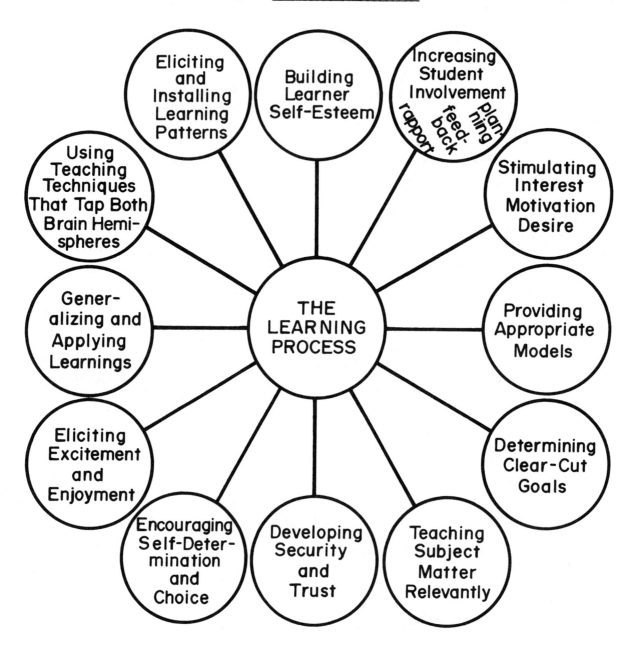

Optimal learning requires knowledge, considerable skill and hard work. (The following comments trace the "spokes" or topics on the "learning wheel." Underlined portions of a sentence indicate when a new topic is being discussed.) High learner self-esteem is an important part of any good learning situation. Student self-esteem can be nurtured by creating a positive environment, by using specific exercises, (see Canfield and Wells, 100 Ways to Enhance Self-Esteem), and by using some of the techniques found in this book. Research and individual experience has indicated that those students who are involved in planning learning activities tend to be more highly motivated than are those who do not have such a choice. Establishing rapport with students is an important part of becoming a "Master Teacher", and how this is accomplished is described in detail later in this book. Modeling human behavior is a part of personality development. Teachers are frequently used as models, or as model comparisons, for students' personality development. There is no substitute for clear-cut instructional goals. Students need to know subject matter goals. Coupled with goals, subject matter, whenever possible, needs to be presented in a manner that is relevant or interesting and that in some way touches upon the world of the student. Establishing security and trust between teacher and student plus the possibility of determining some of one's learning experiences or at least having some choices in the matter can lead to increased excitement and enjoyment in learning. In addition, learnings need to be generalized and teaching techniques need to tap both brain hemispheres. An important part of accelerating the learning process is to learn techniques that determine the sequence and order of visual, auditory, kinesthetic, or olfactory/gustatory (smell/taste) learning patterns. How to elicit and to install these learning patterns will be explained in detail in this book.

General Concepts of Communication

Good communication is the essence of superior teaching. Two important concepts that are vital to good communication are the following:

1) **Regardless of your intention, the meaning in your communication is the response that you receive.**

   There are no mistakes in communication, there are only responses and outcomes. If you are unable to get the responses from your students that you seek, then change your communication pattern.

2) **The purpose of good communication is to act effectively.**

   In this instance, "good communication" means that the teacher changes the student's state so that he is more receptive to the teaching and learning process. To "act effectively" means to do everything in one's power to keep the student in a receptive state. Teachers tend to use techniques to keep students in receptive states that have worked well in the past. Over a period of time, those once useful techniques may lose their effectiveness. A switch to new techniques, despite having to make adjustments, will result in teachers "acting effectively." More information explaining what is meant by "receptive states" immediately follows in the "Principles of Learning" section.

The "Principles of Learning"

Dovetailing with these general communication concepts are four "Principles of Learning".

Principle #1: **In order for superior communication to occur, the development of a physiological state that allows maximum communication to occur is necessary.**

For learning to occur, students need to be in an optimum physiological state. The student's physical appearance, including posture, facial expression, eye movements, breathing patterns, voice tone and tempo, provides information about whether the student is in a state that is conducive to learning.

A student's internal state correlates with his physiology. One can be changed and the other automatically changes. It is much easier to change the student's physiological state than it is to change his internal state. Therefore, a major objective of all teachers should be to get and to keep students in an optimum physiological state that is conducive to learning.

Principle #2:   **In any teaching-learning situation, the person with the most flexibility ends up controlling the situation.**

Flexibility may involve regarding a situation from different points of view or it may involve the ability to respond to various situations in a number of different but appropriate ways. When something is not working, change is necessary. The more experienced teacher will generally feel more secure about changing teaching methodologies and/or techniques on short notice than will a less experienced teacher. Nevertheless, striving to be more creative and spontaneous when one's best-laid teaching plans are not working is more than highly desirable, it is necessary!

An extension of this "Principle" is the statement: student resistance to communication is an indication of inflexibility on the part of the teacher. To state it another way, flexible and skillful communication can overcome student resistance.

Principle #3:   **A student's highest quality response is always behavioral.**

The ability to see, hear, and feel (sensory acuity), what is occurring in the communication interaction that takes place with one's students is imperative because tuning into the sensory feedback of the student provides evidence of the state of the individual and whether he has achieved the physiological state that is essential for learning to take place. Sensory feedback is the best method of determining if students have achieved the physiological state desired by the teacher.

Communication, by its very nature, strives to influence another's experiences. Learning to develop "clear" sensory channels will allow for more "influencing" or teaching to occur and, consequently, will lead to increased learning.

Principle #4:   **Regardless of how it is perceived by you or anyone else, each student's behavior represents the best choice that student has in that situation or at that point in time.**

A student's behavior is a statement about that student's flexibility and about the alternatives available to him in a particular situation and at a particular time. With the techniques in this book, teachers can help draw upon previously untapped resources to find more positive alternative responses to a particular stimulus or situation.

How to Use This Book

Master Teaching Techniques presents information and concepts in a unique manner. For the reader, this approach includes learning the techniques through a sensory-based series of exercises, along with reading this book to obtain information in the conventional cognitive manner. Trainers of many types of information and skills now contend that sensory-based learning of techniques is superior to traditional cognitive learning! This belief is due to the fact that cognitive learning usually results in little, if any, behavioral change. Behavioral reorganization, which is achieved through sensory-based learning, also results in cognitive reorganization.

Most of the sections of this book are deliberately reduced in size so that the information in the sections can be more easily learned. Practice activities accompany many of the chapters, as do sensory-based exercises. Consequently, if your purpose in reading this book is to integrate this knowledge and these techniques into your teaching repertoire, then team up with two adults, practice the sensory-based exercises, and do the collateral exercises as you read the chapters.

Throughout this book I have referred to the student as "he", since constant use of "he or she" is awkward. The terms "student", "individual", and "person", are in reality interchangeable because although this book advocates the use of techniques with students, the techniques obviously can be used with non-students as well. Also, at points where I felt it was needed, I have included sections discussing how best to apply the techniques to elementary students.

Acknowledgments

I wish to thank the following people for their assistance: Pam Coleman, Jeanne Dugdale, Leona Armstrong, Kathy Ericsen, Dr. Kelly Conrad, Dr. Rick Bauman and Dr. Robert Pavlik. The constructive suggestions, given by teachers who have read the forerunner of this book (Master Teaching) as a class assignment, have not only been appreciated, but many of them have been incorporated in this present volume.

SECTION ONE

The Structure of Learning

Chapter 1

OVERVIEW

Once upon a time there were two cities located across the river from each other, connected by an old bridge. People frequently needed to travel from one city to the other for entertainment purposes, for supplies, to visit their friends and to go to work. For years people had used the old bridge and had been well pleased with its performance. However, as times changed and the automobile traffic increased across the bridge, some people called for a new bridge, saying that the old one was too narrow, it was in need of improvement, it was too costly to fix and that it was an eyesore. After much discussion and deliberation, the representatives of the taxpayers decided in favor of a new bridge. Much planning went into the building of the structure, and the bridge was under construction for several years. The construction forced people to utilize new approaches to the old bridge, which took some adjustment on the part of the people using the bridge. Those who were particularly set in using the old ways were frustrated and often confused about which streets to use to gain access to the bridge. Those who had been opposed to the new bridge all along pointed to the confusion and frustration and said, "We would all have been better off if we had kept the old bridge." Finally the new bridge was completed. Many favorable comments were heard about the appearance of the bridge and how well it served its function. More and more, people realized that there were valid reasons to cross the bridge to get to the other city, and that now it was easier to do so. The traffic between the two cities increased, and both cities became more prosperous. People from both cities felt good about being progressive in their ideas and in their actions. The old bridge had served its purpose and was demolished. However, a few people still tried to cross the river where the old bridge had been.

What is the purpose of Section 1? What is learning? What is "chunking" and how does this apply to teaching? What does the phrase "each person has his own model of the world" mean? Why are students' sensory clues important? What are ways that "state change" can be achieved?

Section 1 provides information about how students learn, and how they process information. Specific information is discussed in this section for these four purposes:

<u>Understanding that students process information visually, auditorily and kinesthetically.</u>

<u>Relating student predicate patterns to their sensory systems.</u>

<u>Realizing that students' sensory cues such as eye movement patterns, body posture, gestures, breathing, and voice tone and tempo provide information about their learning patterns.</u>

<u>Knowing that brain hemispheric function relates to student learning styles and that this impacts teaching efforts.</u>

Learning

In its educational context, the word "learning" is generally defined as "the act of acquiring knowledge or skill," or "knowledge or skills that are obtained by observation, study, or instruction." Teachers make reasonable efforts to ensure that their teaching leads to learning. The varying degrees of success and the attempts to achieve consistent and predictable behavior in students frequently tend to be sporadic - a "hit and miss" affair. Master Teaching Techniques gives teachers the opportunity to make teaching performances consistent, positive and high quality experiences. Learning becomes the norm rather than the exception!

"Chunking"

One decision makes it difficult for consistent teaching to occur: how much information to present to students at any one time. How to make this decision was the subject of a now classic paper entitled, "The Magical Number Seven, Plus or Minus Two," written in 1956 by George Miller. According to Miller, people can deal with seven, plus or minus two, chunks of information consciously and comfortably. More than nine chunks of information can lead to confusion and overload. Less than five chunks of information results in inefficient use of our mind and can lead to boredom.

Miller was vague regarding what constitutes a "chunk" of knowledge. Yet, his theory stated that proper organization of information puts knowledge into suitable "chunk size" so that it can be absorbed easily by the student. Information can be "chunked down" by breaking a complex body of information and/or skills into smaller, more easily learned segments. The student can "chunk up" information by tying a body of information, skills and generalizations to a larger frame or context.

Persons overwhelmed by a task "chunk down" by finding a "chewable chunk" or a "workable amount" so that the person doesn't focus all of his cognitive abilities on the whole task but just on those parts that he can handle well. "Chunking up" occurs after the smaller segments have been learned. The person masters all of the parts and can begin to put them together in different ways to adjust to different contexts. The difference between "chunking up" and "chunking down" can be illustrated in the example of a person learning to drive a car. The prospective driver becomes conscious of many smaller parts or "chunks" that he needs to master before he can drive. These chunks include executing a number of mechanical skills, watching the speedometer and the dashboard gauges, as well as watching the traffic flow and the road signs. A great deal of effort and practice precedes meshing everything together. The identification and mastery of these parts is the "chunking down" process. The meshing process which enables the person to drive is an example of "chunking up". In this example "chunking down" provides the vital link so that "chunking up" can occur.

Other examples where "chunking down" and "chunking up" occur include learning to type, playing a musical instrument, and solving math problems. When learning to type or play a musical instrument, a person thinks through the prerequisite skills or the parts that go into the overall process. The person recognizes in a general sense what he needs to know and works with these parts before putting them back together as a whole. The math student who has assimilated a number of methods for solving certain math problems is preparing his mind for future problem solving. He has "chunked down" to learn these methods. When he is presented with a new but similar problem, he "chunks up" by automatically and unconsciously choosing the best method from his background to solve the problem.

A final example of chunking is associated with the purpose that a person has when choosing a particular behavior. The teacher unhappy with the results of a test could examine his teaching techniques or his testing techniques to determine if they are satisfying his purpose(s). For example, a teacher could have used an objective test which would be an attempt to "chunk down", to measure his students' knowledge of the reasons leading to World War I. The test could have yielded only specific elements of information memorized by the students. A better choice in this situation, depending on the teacher's intention, might be to use an essay test which would encourage students to "chunk up" and integrate specific pieces of information to demonstrate their total understanding of the subject matter.

Chunking naturally occurs when any academic area such as math, or history is understood and mastered. Anytime a student attempts to learn a large body of knowledge and feels overwhelmed, "chunking down" will enable him to learn the material at a comfortable level. Mastering the subject matter at a particular level, the student can "chunk up" or build upon and expand his achievements until instructional goals have been met. Teachers facing student questions about the value or need of learning subject matter would do well to "chunk up" and connect the subject matter to the students' lives.

Efficient learners continually process chunks of information in an effort to absorb, store, or learn them. Some comparisons can be made between our awareness of the small percentage of an iceberg that appears above the surface of the ocean (10%) and an awareness of our total learning efforts. Most learners are only aware of their conscious efforts to chunk information. These efforts represent a small percentage of their total learning efforts. Most of the iceberg lies beneath the water and a significant amount of our learning occurs on the unconscious level. The efficient learner is one who is becoming more and more conscious of the chunking behaviors that normally occur unconsciously.

Our experiences help us to develop learning patterns for processing information. Behavior patterns emerge and refine these strategies and experiences. These patterns are then stored unconsciously while we deal with other information. However, recognizing the wisdom of Miller's thoughts about organizing material into five to nine chunks and developing an awareness of "chunking up" or "down" can lead to more evenly paced teaching and learning.

Each Person Has His Own Model Of The World

Our unique experiences provide each of us with our own private perception of, or model of the real world. For example, Sally's perception, or "model," can view a glass half filled with water as being "half full." Bill's perception or "model" can see the same glass as "half empty." An inexperienced teacher's "model of the world" can view a student having difficulty learning new material as that child's problem. However, a master teacher's "model of the world" would see the child's inability to learn new material as a teaching problem, rather than as a learning problem.

To understand how people create their own models of the world, think of your colleagues. Some are more subject matter-oriented than student-oriented and vice versa. Strict subject matter-oriented teachers would view students as vessels to be filled with knowledge and information. Strict student-oriented teachers, if faced with the choice between helping an individual student solve a personal crisis or teaching that student subject matter, would opt for resolving the crisis. These are examples of educators who have different models of the world.

Students also have different models of the world. Some view school predominantly as a social event, others view it as preparation for college, some see it as a combination of the two and some students perceive it as vocational training for a job. Another example of different models of the world would be a coach who views participation in his sport as an enjoyable character-building experience, while another coach of the same sport sees participation in his sport as an extension of his need to win and to prove himself. So it is that our creation or perception of the real world differs from another's perception. Thus the phrase, "Each person has his own model of the world."

Changing Students' States

Teachers often need to change the physical and/or psychological states of their students to prepare them for learning. Researchers over the last three decades have discovered that students' internal states and physiology influence one another. However in preparing students to learn, it is easier to alter students' physiologies than internal states. Fourteen of many ways to change students' internal states appear below:

1) Change the Subject - The teacher either creates a break in the conversation, or waits for a natural break. Then, he switches to another topic.

2) Use Humor - One-liners, humorous stories or incidents can bring about rapid state changes. The teacher can build on the topic or thrust of the one-liner, or he can use humor as a state change and then continue with his planned lesson.

3) Direct Contact - Most teachers and students feel comfortable making direct contact - or touching - when it is done in "context." Teachers know which students can be touched and the kind of touch that is appropriate: a hand on the shoulder, a touch on the arm, a touch on the elbow.

4) Switch Roles - The teacher says, "I don't seem to be able to reach you. Show me what I should do to reach you." or "If you were me, what would you do differently?" or "I wonder if we switch roles if you could show me how to teach this lesson to you. Let's do that. I'll be you and you be me. Show me how I could best teach you."

5) Employ "My Friend John" - This technique can be used when a particular state change is desired, but the teacher does not wish to take responsibility for the change. The teacher says, "I've never done this experiment before, but my friend John would do this ..." The teacher carries out the action which is designed to create the desired change(s). For example, in a situation where most of the class is not responding to the lesson presentation the teacher says, "It looks like this lesson is boring you to death. I'm going to do what my friend John, who is an excellent teacher, would do. He would ask you for suggestions about how we could make this lesson more interesting. What suggestions would you have?" A state change occurs as a result of the interaction, and the students are moved toward a physiological state more conducive to learning.

6) Pretend to Quote Other People - A teacher uses a "pretended quote" to send a message containing a built-in state change to a student, but this technique allows the teacher to give someone else the credit for the statement. For example, the teacher wishes to change the state of a student who is showing signs of falling asleep after lunch. The teacher says to the student: "The darndest thing happened to me this morning. I was feeling sleepy and almost walked into another teacher. He said to me, 'Why don't you wake up!' (with loud voice). I didn't know how to react. How would you have reacted?" The effect of any "pretended quote" message is enhanced if it is delivered in close

proximity to the student. The teacher conveyed his intended message to the student, and the student should show signs of rapid state change without creating a serious conflict.

7) Ask for the Students' Assistance - Many students like to become involved in assisting a teacher in developing a lesson, so requesting assistance can result in a positive change of state. Comments like, "Bill, I'd like to brain-storm some ways to present this lesson so that you would find it interesting. Would you help me do that?"

8) Play Incompetent - Another suitable maneuver for some situations and for some students, is having the teacher play incompetent. "I'm really not exactly sure how to do this ... etc." This state change plays on the fact that students enjoy showing others that they can contribute to the learning experience. It can create involvement and, therefore, a state change.

9) Give Up - This state change has to be used selectively. In some situations, the teacher may want to pretend to give up. "I just don't seem to be able to teach you. I guess I'm just a failure." etc. This state change is based on the idea that people generally don't want to see others fail, and a positive behavioral change could result if used with selected students and in selected situations.

10) Move or Cause Body Change - Causing or having students move or change their body position effectively changes their state. Students could stand up and stretch, breath deeply, go for a walk, and switch to different activities.

11) Assign A Task - Examples of assigning tasks are to ask students to write on the blackboard, or to look up some information in the encyclopedia, or to borrow an item from another teacher, or to reorganize the book shelves.

12) Change Rhythm and Tempo - Lowering one's volume or changing one's tone, or slowing one's tempo can change the state of learning. Shouting matches can be defused by lowering one's voice volume and tone, and by slowing down the tempo of the conversation. A student can "hear" better if the teacher speaks more slowly and evenly. Most teachers effectively change the rhythm, tempo and volume of their voice to capture and maintain the attentiveness of their students.

13) Use Embedded Commands - The teacher has a command embedded in a seemingly harmless statement. "An interested student knows how to pay attention, Bob." or "Jane, if you can imagine yourself finishing your assignment and how relieved it will make you feel, you will want to complete your assignment!" The voice tone is changed where the sentence is underlined, thus making the statement more of a command. This technique will stimulate the student's unconscious, and the desired state change may result.

14) Be Honest - The teacher makes a statement such as, "I'm really having a very difficult time teaching you this information.", or "How can I show you this problem so you will understand it?", or "How can I reword this definition so you'll understand it?", etc. This technique opens up the possibility of resolving the situation through a discussion.

Sensory Clues

Students can give us clues about how they process subject matter: visually, auditorily or kinesthetically. One such clue is the predicate patterns the students use. Some students tend to be visually oriented:

"I see what you're getting at."
"I can picture that."

Others are auditorily oriented:

"I hear what you're saying."
"We are in harmony."

Some are kinesthetically oriented:

"I'm really getting a firm grip on this information."
"I like concrete examples."

Other helpful clues are involuntary eye movement patterns, posture and muscle tone changes, tonal and tempo changes, changes in facial skin coloring, and breathing patterns.

Sensory awareness is the key to becoming a master teacher. Any attempt to move the student toward an instructional goal, or desired physiological state, or a personal outcome may be gauged as successful or unsuccessful by the sensory clues that the student exhibits. This point cannot be emphasized too strongly! The difference between a skilled person and an unskilled person using the formalized change procedures in this book and being successful, rests on the skilled person's ability to observe and to interpret the students' sensory feedback.

Sensory Exercises

At the end of most chapters, a number of exercises have been presented to assist you in developing your sensory acuity and to encourage you to be more aware of your communication patterns. The exercises will also encourage flexibility, an important characteristic of a master teacher. Unless otherwise indicated, most of the exercises require three people. Select two adults to work with who are readily accessible over a period of time. Each exercise takes approximately fifteen minutes to complete. For effective integration to occur, participants should take as much time as they need to complete each exercise. After each exercise, discuss the insights and discoveries you experienced. The exercises are designed to be completed in sequence.

The collateral exercises act as a bridge between the sensory based exercises and transferring those awarenesses to your students.

Exercise #1
Auditory and Tonal Discovery

Purpose: To sharpen one's auditory senses.

Decide who is 'A', 'B' & 'C'.

'A' closes his eyes.

'B' & 'C' choose a sound (clicking tongue, snapping fingers, or clapping hands).

Each person takes turns making the sound and identifying who made it. (Example: "click," Susan; "click", Amy).

When 'A' has correlated the sounds with the voices, 'B' & 'C' make the sounds randomly (without the identifying voices), and 'A' identifies the individual making the sound.

When 'A' has correctly identified the person making the sound four or five times consecutively, then 'B' & 'C' rotate with 'A' & each person takes turns identifying who is making the sounds.

(For those wanting more challenges, after the first time through, repeat the exercise while trying to mimic one another as closely as possible.)

Collateral Exercise #1

Purpose: To transfer one's auditory sensitivity to the classroom.

The teacher selects five students from a classroom or class. He compares the sound of their voices, the tonal quality of their voices, the tempo of their speech pattern, the volume of their voices, and their laughter. What differences are noticed?

(Closing one's eyes may make it easier to complete this exercise.)

Exercise #2
Kinesthetic Discovery

Purpose: To sharpen one's kinesthetic senses.

'A' closes his eyes.

'B' & 'C' touch 'A', again identifying themselves each time they touch 'A'. (Example: A finger in some manner touching the arm, hand, or knee, and then identifying the toucher, "Amy.")

When 'A' has calibrated the touches with the voices, then 'B' & 'C' touch 'A' but without identifying themselves. 'A' is to distinguish between the two touches, (through pressure or temperature), and 'A' is to identify the person doing the touching.

When 'A' has correctly identified the person doing the touching four or five times consecutively, then 'B' and 'C' rotate with 'A' and each person takes turns identifying who is doing the touching.

(A more difficult challenge would be for 'B' & 'C' to touch in the same place, to match the pressure.)

Exercise #3
Visual Discovery

Purpose: To sharpen one's visual senses.

'A' develops a particular posture or stance.

'B' views the posture, then closes his eyes.

'A' changes posture (Make obvious changes to begin with; more subtle changes as expertise develops.)

'B' opens eyes and describes what changes took place.

'C' observes and either confirms or indicates changes which he observed but that 'B' did not see.

After each sequence, rotate the roles.

Collateral Exercise #2

Purpose: To transfer one's kinesthetic sensitivity to the classroom.

The teacher selects five students. They select an item that is symbolic of themselves and place the items on a desk or table. The teacher either has his eyes closed or is blindfolded. He identifies the student by naming the object and matching it to his knowledge of the student.

Collateral Exercise #3

Purpose: To transfer one's visual acuity to the classroom.

The teacher selects several students and notes their posture or stance at the beginning of the class, and at another point during the class. What are the differences?

(Taking a before and after mental snapshot of the students is helpful. Then the snapshots can be compared and the differences noted.)

Exercise #4
Changing States

Purpose: To increase flexibility and to find ways to move students toward a physiological state conducive to learning.

'A' identifies a student state that is difficult for him to deal with.

'A' describes that state to 'B'.

'B' models the state. (If necessary, 'A' coaches.)

'A' takes 5 minutes and attempts to change 'B's state in as many ways as possible. (This exercise demonstrates the importance of flexibility.)

'C' serves as referee and tells 'A' when 'B' has changed state.

Rotate the roles.

Collateral Exercise #4

Purpose: To transfer one's ability to change student states to classroom reality.

The teacher waits for the student state that is difficult for him to deal with to surface in the classroom. When it surfaces, he uses one or more state changes and successfully alters the undesirable state. He then continues on with the planned activity.

SUMMARY

The connection between teaching and learning is greatly facilitated by our ability to be aware of and to understand what is happening to ourselves and to our students as we interact.

The process of "chunking down" and "chunking up" information allows us to provide teaching-learning experiences which better meet both teacher and student needs. An awareness that each person has his own perception of the world, and therefore of the subjects that we teach, should encourage us to be more flexible in our teaching and non-teaching relationships with students.

By consciously being aware of the correlation between physiological states and internal states, we will realize when students are either in or out of desirable learning states and we will be able to more easily take whatever steps are necessary to keep students in those desirable states.

By becoming consciously attuned to students' sensory feedback, we will have a better understanding of how students process information. With the realization of the need to develop and use teaching activities that teach to both brain hemispheres, learning can become an easier experience for many students and we will find teaching to be a more rewarding experience than we previously imagined!

Chapter 2

SENSORY SYSTEMS

The Master viewed the jigsaw puzzle with interest. Quickly he selected the outside edges and outlined the puzzle. He then divided the puzzle into segments according to color and isolated the various colors. He scanned the individual pieces in each color segment and quickly put each section together. Then he joined the sections together, completing the puzzle in record time.

The Master surveyed his classroom. He had established his teaching goals and the desired physiological states that he sought for his pupils. He acquired information about the states of his pupils by observing, listening and processing his feelings about his feedback. He noted that while his students used all of their senses in the learning process, most students relied on one sense to process information and to provide behavioral feedback to others. The Master took this information into account, orchestrated his instruction providing visual, auditory and kinesthetic segments in each lesson, thus making the lesson complete and ensuring the achievement of both his instructional goals and the physiological states he desired for his students. His title of "Master" was well-deserved!

**How do bodily senses affect our ability to perceive the world differently?
What impact do sensory systems have on the learning process?**

Our brain continually processes information through our five sensory systems. Our ability to see, hear, feel, taste and smell, allows this processing of information to occur both consciously and unconsciously. Figure I describes the sensory systems and the coding process which will be consistently used throughout this book.

Fig. I: The Sensory System & Their Codes

Sensory System			Coding
Visual (sight; V)		V^i –	refers to visual internal sources, or general images that we construct or remember.
		V^e –	denotes visual external sources, or what we see externally.
	*	V^c –	represents visual images that we construct.
	*	V^r –	indicates a remembered image.
Auditory (hearing; A)		A^i –	refers to general sounds that we construct or remember.
		A^e –	denotes auditory external sounds that we hear.
	*	A^c –	represents internal or external sounds that we construct.

	* A^r	indicates a remembered sound.
	* A_d^i	denotes an internal dialogue.
Kinesthetic (body sensation – K)	* K^i	refers to internal feelings that we construct or remember.
	* K^e	denotes external feelings that we experience.
	K^c	represents internal or external feelings that we construct.
	K^r	indicates a remembered internal or external feeling.
Olfactory/Gustatory (smell/taste – O)	O^i	refers to smells or tastes that we construct or remember.
	O^e	denotes external smells or tastes that we experience.
	O^c	represents internal or external smells or tastes that we construct.
	O^r	indicates a remembered internal or external smell and/or taste.

Our sensory systems represent the ways in which we perceive, learn, initiate and model behavior. Our model of our experiences is a direct result of the processing that occurs in our sensory systems.

All of the sensory systems together (V, A, K, O) are referred to as a "sensory set". Our brain constantly monitors information in every channel of our sensory experience at any particular moment. When we teach, for example, we see the room and the students, which is external (V^e), while simultaneously we internally visualize or remember the lesson being taught (V^r). Auditorily, we may hear the students reciting (A^e), but internally we could be thinking about the next steps of the lesson (A_d^i) or comparing a students' present statement (A^e) to one we remember the student making in the past (A^r). Kinesthetically we may feel the exterior sensation of our feet touching the floor, our fingers grasping the chalk as we write on the blackboard, the touch of our clothes on our bodies (K^e), but internally we may be feeling hunger pangs or sensing that all is not right with a particular student (K^i). Olfactorily, we may be smelling the scent of a flower in the room (O^e), but internally we may be remembering the way the food smells that is listed on the day's cafeteria menu (O^r). Figure 2 summarizes this external and internal information.

---

*These codes are most commonly used.

Fig. 2: Identifying Sensory Systems In A Specific Teaching Context

	External	Internal
Visual	view the room & students (V^e)	visualizing the lesson (V^r)
Auditory	hear the students (A^e)	stating to self the next steps of the lesson (A_d^i) or remembering the sound of a student making a past statement (A^r)
Kinesthetic	feel feet touch floor (K^e)	feel hunger pangs (K^i)
Olfactory/ Gustatory	smell flower (O^e)	remember the smell of food (O^r)

Figure 2 helps to illustrate the fact that we consistently tend to experience "mixed states." Some of our experience is external, while we simultaneously experience remembered or fantasized incidents. An awareness of the number of possible "mixed states" that each of us entertains in one learning experience helps us to understand why each person's model of the world will be unique.

Dominant Sensory Systems

While information is collected through all of our sensory systems, each of us has a tendency to process information and to initiate our behavioral feedback through one or more selected sensory systems. The sensory system or systems that are most within our consciousness will be referred to as "dominant" sensory systems. A reliable way to determine an individual's dominant sensory system(s) is by listening to his predicate patterns. By proceeding through the sensory exercises at the end of most chapters each reader will "discover" his dominant sensory system(s). It is possible that the "dominant" sensory system can differ from context to context.

Knowing that each person has his own "dominant" sensory system can help us understand how each person perceives the real world differently. This knowledge also helps explain why some students find learning one subject easier than another. The visual learner will probably have less difficulty learning math than will the student whose most dominant sensory system is kinesthetic. In an example illustrating this statement, Dilts discusses the case of a special education student with a dominant kinesthetic sensory system who had difficulty working algebra problems either on the blackboard or on paper. A blind student, also in the same class, solved the same math problem by using algebraic materials developed in braille. The teacher taught the kinesthetically-oriented student to learn the braille system. He was then able to use the braille system (which appealed to his kinesthetic orientation) and he learned algebra much more rapidly than previously. (Dilts, Neuro-Linguistic Programming, Vol. I, p.153) A good musician has to be able to hear the notes. A dancer must be able to encode kinesthetically.

This information also helps to explain why some students tend to be "talented" in such areas as acting, music or athletics. A person's dominant sensory system is compatible with learning a certain skill or expertise as a result of certain physiological developments (genetic inheritance, etc.) and environmental circumstances. For example, a person's genetic make-up may enable him to have an inherent accurate sense of pitch.

This ability can be developed by opportunities in his environmental circumstance and he may become a gifted musician. Consequently, a talented person begins to emerge if the necessary experiences build a programming that allow a person to combine his dominant sensory system with the new learning skill. If placed in learning experiences that are predominately non-auditory, this student would probably not learn to the best of his ability. Some classroom disruptions are probably caused by the teacher presenting lessons in a sensory system that differs from the dominant sensory system used by the student to process information.

The following table contains a list of observable characteristics for each of the dominant sensory systems of students.[1]

Table 1: Behavior Characteristics Identifying
Students' Dominant Sensory Systems

	Visual	**Auditory**	**Kinesthetic**
Learning Style	Learns by seeing; watching demonstrations	Learns through verbal instructions from others or self	Learns by doing; direct involvement
Reading	Likes description; sometimes stops reading to stare into space and imagine scene; intense concentration	Enjoys dialogue, plays; avoids lengthy description unaware of illustrations; moves lips or subvocalizes	Prefers stories where action occurs early; fidgets when reading, handles books; not an avid reader
Spelling	Recognizes words by sight; relies on configuration of words	Uses a phonics approach; has auditory word attack skills	Often is a poor speller; writes words to determine if they "feel" right
Handwriting	Tends to be good, particularly when young; spacing and size are good; appearance is important	Has more difficulty learning in initial stages; tends to write lightly; says strokes when writing	Good initially, deteriorates when space becomes smaller; pushes harder on writing instrument
Memory	Remembers faces, forgets names; writes things down, takes notes	Remembers names, forgets faces; remembers by auditory repetition	Remembers best what was done, not what was seen or talked about
Imagery	Vivid imagination; thinks in pictures, visualizes in detail	Subvocalizes, thinks in sounds; details less important	Imagery not important; images that do occur are accompanied by movement
Distractibility	Generally unaware of sounds; distracted by visual disorder or movement	Easily distracted by sounds	Not attentive to visual, auditory presentation so seems distractible
Problem Solving	Deliberate; plans in advance; organizes thoughts by writing them; lists problems	Talks problems out, tries solutions verbally, subvocally; talks self through problem	Attacks problems physically; impulsive; often selects solution involving greatest activity

(Continued)

[1]From Teaching Through Modality Strengths: Concepts and Practices, c. 1979, Zaner-Bloser, Inc., Reprinted by permission. The authors of this book also have published an instrument to measure modality strengths.

	Visual	Auditory	Kinesthetic
Response to Periods of Inactivity	Stares; doodles; finds something to watch	Hums; talks to self or to others	Fidgets; finds reasons to move; holds up hand
Response to New Situations	Looks around; examines structure	Talks about situation, pros and cons, what to do	Tries things out; touches, feels; manipulates
Emotionality	Somewhat repressed; stares when angry; cries easily, beams when happy; facial expression is a good index of emotion	Shouts with joy or anger; blows up verbally but soon calms down; expresses emotion verbally and through changes in tone, volume, pitch of voice	Jumps for joy; hugs, tugs, and pulls when happy; stamps, jumps, and pounds when angry, stomps off; general body tone is a good index of emotion
Communication	Quiet; does not talk at length; becomes impatient when extensive listening is required; may use words clumsily; describes without embellishment; uses words such as *see, look,* etc.	Enjoys listening but cannot wait to talk; descriptions are long but repetitive; likes hearing self and others talk; uses words such as *listen, hear,* etc.	Gestures when speaking; does not listen well; stands close when speaking or listening; quickly loses interest in detailed verbal discourse; uses words such as *get, take,* etc.
General Appearance	Neat, meticulous, likes order; may choose not to vary appearance	Matching clothes not so important, can explain choices of clothes	Neat but soon becomes wrinkled through activity
Response to the Arts	Not particularly responsive to music; prefers the visual arts; tends not to voice appreciation of art of any kind, but can be deeply affected by visual displays; focuses on details and components rather than the work as a whole	Favors music; finds less appeal in visual art, but is readily able to discuss it; misses significant detail, but appreciates the work as a whole; is able to develop verbal association for all art forms; spends more time talking about pieces than looking at them	Responds to music by physical movement; prefers sculpture; touches statues and paintings; at exhibits stops only at those in which he or she can become physically involved; comments very little on any art form

Each of us has observed classrooms that reflect the dominant sensory system (V,A,K) of the teacher. Use the following practice activity to determine your sensitivity to the activities and/or characteristics that would typically involve visual, auditory and kinesthetically oriented teachers.

Practice Activity A: Using the letters V, A or K, label the activity or characteristic most appropriate for the classroom of the visual, auditory or kinesthetically oriented teacher. (Answers appear in the Appendix on p.224.)

Example:	_A_	lecture used
	K	role playing emphasized
	A	student talk encouraged
	V	bulletin boards decorated
	V	filmstrips and movies shown
	A	audio tapes played
	K	activities requiring manipulation utilized
	V	materials neatly organized
	V	written work stressed
	A	reading aloud expected
	K	student-made projects & models assigned
	V	posters & signs displayed
	V	chalkboard heavily used
	A	math flashcards & examples & answers read aloud
	V	daily work schedule listed on board
	V	desks face teacher
	K	learning aids 3-dimensional & manipulative

As each person tends to rely on a dominant sensory system, we can assume that most teachers tend to favor teaching from their dominant sensory system. This practice could obviously be detrimental for students having a different dominant sensory system because these students would have more difficulty learning the subject matter. For optimum teaching and learning to occur, teachers need to select materials or to develop activities within students' dominant sensory systems. A teacher aware of the dominant sensory systems of his students can capitalize on student strengths and develop weaker sensory systems. For example, a student with a dominant visual sensory system will be less distracted if he is seated where there is less movement. The same student will benefit from any visual learning activities. In communicating with others, the visual student needs exercises to help him be a better listener and to help him learn to more effectively express himself. (Similar types of conclusions can be drawn by carefully examining the areas included in Table I.) A well-rounded instructional format would include demonstrations, outlines, diagrams, additional visual aids (V), lectures and discussions (A), and activities requiring class participation (K). This format coupled with the judicious use of metaphors and predicates will result in the student integrating the educational experiences in all of his sensory systems, thus ensuring the success of the instructional effort.

Exercise #5
Visual & Kinesthetic Discovery

Purpose: To enhance one's visual and kinesthetic acuity.

'A' visually relives three experiences in his mind that actually happened to him. (Examples: talking to someone, participating in a sporting event, walking, etc.)

'B' faces 'A' and holds 'A's hands (both stand).

As 'A', relives each experience, he squeezes 'B's hands to convey to 'B' when he is in a different experience.

'A' repeats the same three experiences.

'A' then places the experiences in a different order and 'B' is to guess the order of the experiences after all three have been relived.

'C' observes and verifies if 'B' is correct.

'A' again repeats the experiences in their original order and 'B' is to attempt to guess the content of each experience.

Exercise #6
Visual, Auditory & Kinesthetic Discovery (triad or dyad)

Purpose: To enhance one's visual, auditory & kinesthetic acuity by determining the authenticity of each experience.

'A' selects and tells about three experiences: two that 'A' has actually done, and one that 'A' wishes that he could do, but can't or hasn't (this should be realistic; no Mars or moon trips).

'B' determines which experience did not occur.

'C', (if this is a triad), can also try to determine which experience did not occur.

(Continued)

Collateral Exercise #5

Purpose: To transfer one's visual & kinesthetic acuity to the classroom.

The teacher draws a birdseye diagram or sketch of his first classroom. He marks an X where he had his desk. He remembers an experience that occurred in that first year. He visualizes himself in that experience and steps into that experience. The teacher remembers the internal and external feelings that he had at that time. He remembers how he held and positioned his body.

The teacher draws a birdseye diagram of his present classroom. He marks an X where he has his desk. He selects a similar experience as before and remembers the internal and external feelings that he had at that time. The teacher remembers how he positioned his body. He notes any differences in his room arrangement. He remembers how that made him feel. Any differences in the way he now positions his body are recorded. Any differences in his internal and external feelings when compared with the first experience are remembered.

Collateral Exercise #6

Purpose: To transfer visual, auditory & kinesthetic acuity to the classroom.

The teacher selects two or more students. One at a time they draw a birdseye sketch of a previous classroom. With an X they mark a spot where they had a positive experience. They think about the experience without describing it. The teacher observes their sensory feedback. The students next mark a spot where they had a negative experience. The teacher observes their sensory feedback.

(Continued)

Exercise #6
Visual, Auditory & Kinesthetic Discovery (triad or dyad)
(Continued)

Discuss what distinctions you used to determine the real stories.

Rotate the roles.

Collateral Exercise #6
(Continued)

The students select another positive or a negative experience and mark the spot where it happened. The teacher identifies which experience the student has selected. The student verifies the answer.

To make the exercise more challenging, the teacher instructs the student to select experiences that emotionally are more closely aligned.

Exercise #7
Auditory-Kinesthetic Discovery

Purpose: To enhance one's auditory and kinesthetic acuity.

'A' closes his eyes.

'B' makes a sound, then touches 'A' and identifies self.

'C' does the same.

'A' calibrates the sounds and touches with each person, then 'A' is to guess whether 'B' or 'C' has made the sounds and done the touching. 'B' and 'C' should first make obvious sounds and touches, but should make them more subtle as the exercise progresses.

After 'A' has identified the combinations correctly for four or five times consecutively, then 'B' and 'C' can mix the sounds and touches, and 'A' can then identify who has made the sound and who has done the touching.

Rotate the roles when four or five consecutive combinations have been accurately identified.

Collateral Exercise #7

Purpose: To transfer one's auditory and kinesthetic acuity to the classroom.

The teacher selects several students who in turn select an object symbolizing themselves. The teacher either closes his eyes or is blindfolded. The students agree on a word or tone among themselves. Each student, one at a time, makes the tone or says the word, hands the object to the teacher, and identifies himself.

The teacher calibrates to these students and identifies the students four or five times consecutively.

To make the exercise more challenging, the students mix the sounds and the objects and the teacher identifies the student who has made the sound and the one who handed the object to the teacher.

Sensory System Classroom Assessment

While you are in your room, make a sensory system assessment of your classroom by answering the questions that follow. Feel free to add questions that incorporate your special circumstances.

1) What is the color(s) of your room?

2) How does that color(s) make you feel?

3) What senses are stimulated by the pictures and/or posters in your room?

4) What senses are stimulated by your bulletin board materials?

5) What parts of your room are best for:

    -visual centers?

    -auditory centers?

    -kinesthetic centers?

    On what basis have you made your decision?

6) List the visual aids you normally use in your subject-matter presentations.

7) List the auditory aids that you normally use in your subject-matter presentations.

8) List the kinesthetic aids that you normally use in your subject-matter presentations.

9) How does the earth's rotation influence the sun's reflections on your chalkboard? How does it reflect on the need for shades in your classroom? Does the sun affect your classroom in any other way(s)?

10) How loudly, or softly, do students need to talk to be heard, or not heard when sitting in various parts of the room? Are there any "dead" spots in your room?

11) Where can you stand and talk normally so everyone can hear?

12) What part of the room is best for small groups? Why?

13) Walk around your classroom when it is empty. Do parts of the room have different smells?

14) Walk around your classroom and notice if the temperature varies.

15) What visual, auditory and kinesthetic words, or inferences, are incorporated in your classroom rules? ... in your subject-matter directions?

16) What type of visual, auditory & kinesthetic activities do you assign your students?

Summary

The importance of sensory systems in the educational process has been the subject of this chapter. The sensory systems most used in our culture are visual, auditory and kinesthetic (V, A & K). While students are generally only dimly aware of the fact that they are processing information in several different sensory channels, most students will have a dominant sensory system to deal with the flow of information that descends upon them. This dominant sensory system can be identified through sensory feedback from the student which includes predicate usage. As a result of employing different sensory systems, each of us perceives the world in a particular manner and develops his own model of the world. The "sensory set" (V, A, K, O) , a term used to describe all of the sensory systems together, can serve as a basis from which to begin the study of students' sensory systems.

Chapter 3

PREDICATE PATTERNS AND SENSORY SYSTEMS

A teacher came to the Master to seek his advice about how she could reach a student who was "...literally driving her crazy." The Master asked her to describe to him specifically what she found frustrating about working with this student. "It's like he's operating on a different wave-length.", she said. "I talk to him about his behavior or getting his work done, and it's as though he doesn't hear me even though I know he's listening. I keep getting more frustrated and start talking louder. I'm getting so I can't stand working with him!" The Master replied, "I understand what you are saying. How does he reply to you?" "Well," she continued, "He says he has difficulty picturing what I am saying, that it's not clear to him what I am talking about, and that he doesn't see what I'm aiming at." It was evident to the Master that at least part of the teacher's difficulty was due to the fact that she and her student were processing information differently, she auditorily, and he visually. He could tell this by their predicate usage. After the Master explained this fact and demonstrated to her how to increase communication and understanding with that student by matching his predicate patterns, she later reported that this one bit of knowledge opened up new avenues of communication between not only that student, but several other students as well! "This student is actually becoming one of my favorite students!," she enthusiastically stated.

What are "Predicate Patterns?" How do they identify dominant sensory systems? Why should teachers learn to match the "Predicate Patterns" of their students?

Even though an individual may not be aware of it, all parts of a sensory set, (V, A, K, O) are present every time information is processed. In many instances there will be one sensory system that dominates the others. The dominant sensory system can be determined through the predicate patterns that a person uses. This chapter explains predicate patterns and provides common words that typically relate to specific sensory systems. Specific suggestions that will aid you in developing expertise in identifying, learning, and applying these patterns are also included in this chapter.

The "predicate" label includes adjectives, verbs, adverbs and other descriptive words. If a student were to use predicates to indicate a visual representation (V), he might say:

"Now I see how you got that answer!"
              or
"I get the picture!"

Auditory representations would be indicated by such statements as:

"That rings a bell!"
              or
"That's music to my ears!"

Statements indicating kinesthetic predicate usage would include:

"I'm really getting a handle on things!"
              or
"What a smooth performance!"

Olfactory/gustatory representations would be employed by such statements as:

"That experience sure leaves a _sweet_ taste in my mouth!"
or
"That's a _fresh_ idea!"

The following are some examples of predicates that are used to signify particular sensory systems.

Fig. 3: Predicate Examples

Visual	Auditory	Kinesthetic	Olfactory/Gustatory
see	hear	warm	taste
aim	listen	soft	salty
visualize	noisy	rough	spicy
perspective	talk	smooth	bitter
watch	harmony	hot	sweet
look	loud	cold	sour
eyeball	music	heavy	fresh
observe	quiet	cool	stale
focus	amplify	slippery	fragrant
show	shout	handle	savor
peek	scream	tight	pungent
glimpse	screech	loose	odor
horizon	clap	firm	smell
picture	yell	pound	smoky

Some predicates are labeled "unspecified" because they do not identify particular sensory systems or because they can be applied to more than one sensory system. Such words include the following:

Fig. 4: Unspecified Predicates

understand	learn
know	nice
believe	remember
think	consider
sense	change
notice	become aware
light (V or K)	respectful
clear (V or A)	trusting

To determine the sensory systems of students using unspecified predicates, simply ask for more information until a sensory description is forthcoming. For example, if a student says, "I don't understand how to solve this problem.," the teacher can ask for more information. "How, specifically, do you not understand it?" Another teacher response would be to use predicates in sentences and gauge the student's feedback. "How could I get you to see how to solve this problem?" or "How could I explain this so it would sound good to you?" or "How could I explain this so that it feels good to you?" Knowing students' dominant sensory systems can provide teachers clues about how best to respond to student use of unspecified predicates.

These activities will help you determine which sensory systems your students use. (Answers to Practice Activities B and D can be found in the Appendix on pages 224 and 225.)

Practice Activity B: Mark each of the phrases in the following list as either visual (V), kinesthetic (K), auditory (A), olfactory/gustatory (O), or unspecified (US).

Example

K	tripped on it	___	think smart
O	that's tart	___	learn quickly
V	bright outlook	___	harmonize here
A	raucous crowd	___	was pressured
___	glimpse of the future	___	in tune
___	a true belief	___	yummy solution
___	sweet on it	___	in focus
___	grasp it	___	stale news
___	loud mouth	___	modulated voice
___	feel changed	___	oily situation
___	colorful ideas	___	ticklish situation
___	quiet person	___	correct perspective

Practice Activity C: Determine for a particular moment in time, the predicates that you use, or the predicates of a friend, student or someone on radio or TV. What are some predicates that predominate? What sensory system is being used? (Record your comments in the blank space.)

Practice Activity D: Identify the sensory system being expressed in each sentence. Then, restate the example matching the original sensory system. Finally, construct two sentences, each of which translates the original response into a different sensory system.

Example: "Now you are warming to your task."

Sensory System Utilized: K

Matching Response: I am really getting a handle on this job.

Translation: I am getting a clear picture of my task. (V)
I am in harmony with my goal. (A)

1. "People usually see me as I see myself."

S.S.U.: ___

M.R.: _____

T.: _____

_____

2. "I need to get in touch with my joy."

S.S.U.: ___

M.R.: _____

T.: _____

_____

3. "I get many fresh ideas."

S.S.U.: ___

M.R.: _____

T.: _____

_____

4. "Things are beginning to click."

S.S.U.: ___

M.R.: _____

T.: _____

_____

5. "This is the real bright spot in my life."

S.S.U.: ___

M.R.: _____

T.: _____

_____

6. "I feel close ties to my family."

S.S.U.: ___

M.R.: _____

T.: _____

_____

An awareness of predicate usage enables a teacher to devise learning activities for one or more students centering around the sensory system pin-pointed by the student's particular predicate usages. For example, if a student used predominately kinesthetic predicates in his speech, the teacher could identify other students using kinesthetic predicates and design a kinesthetic activity, such as role-playing, to meet the needs of those particular students. (It is possible that a student may process information in a different sensory system from the one indicated by his predicate usage. The best way to determine the success of the activity, or of any teaching effort, is to observe the student's sensory feedback.)

The ability to identify and to match various predicates is helpful in establishing clear and more direct communication. This communication occurs because both the teacher and the student are speaking the same language. Although establishing rapport is the subject of Chapter 9, one way in which rapport can be accomplished is by matching students' predicates. In those instances when students use predicates from more than one sensory system, optimum rapport is established if the predicates are matched in the same order in which they were originally given.

For example: Student: "I can see how to do the problem now. I get a good feeling when I hear the right answer and it matches the one on my paper."

Teacher: "Seeing you do the problem correctly makes me feel good, and to listen to you say that is a real treat!"

Exercise #8
Matching Predicates

Purpose: To learn to match predicates in the order they are spoken.

'A' states a sentence with a visual predicate. (Example: "I see the snow blowing in the winter.")

'B' adds an auditory predicate. (Example: "As you see the snow blowing in the winter, you can hear the wind howling.")

(Continued)

Collateral Exercise #8

Purpose: To transfer an awareness of predicate usage to the classroom.

The teacher selects five students and listens to their predicate usage for five days. Do they consistently use predicates from one sensory system? Does their predicate usage vary according to the type of activity they are doing?

'C' adds a kinesthetic predicate. (Example: "As you see the snow blowing in the winter, you can hear the wind howling, and <u>feel</u> the cold.")

Continue, repeating for a second round using the same sentence.

Then rotate the roles.

Exercise #9
Visual and Auditory Discovery

Purpose: To intensify one's visual and auditory acuity and to encourage flexibility.

Phase I

'B' & 'C' face each other and form a particular posture.

'A' looks between 'B' and 'C' and makes a visual snapshot of the postures. 'A' then closes his eyes.

'B' & 'C' resume what would be for them a normal posture.

'A' duplicates the original posture of each.

'B' & 'C' give 'A' feedback.

Rotate the roles.

Phase II

'B' & 'C' - face each other and form a particular posture.

'A' visually registers the postures, then closes his eyes.

'B' & 'C' form a different posture.
(Continued)

Collateral Exercise #9

Purpose: To transfer increased visual and auditory acuity flexibility to the classroom.

The teacher develops several situations that require two students to role-play. The teacher tape records the role-play exercises. He makes a mental snapshot of two of the postures of the students and remembers a short statement made by each student when they were in those postures.

Later, the teacher uses the tape recorder to refresh his memory and he physically duplicates the postures of each student and duplicates their comments at the same time.

Exercise #9
Visual and Auditory Discovery
(Continued)

'A' duplicates the first posture of both 'B' & 'C', and then duplicates the second posture.

'B' & 'C' give 'A' feedback.

Rotate the roles.

Phase III

(This phase may be difficult to do because there is so much information to assimilate, but by redoing this phase several times, it will become easier to execute.)

'B' & 'C' face each other, form a particular posture and add a short statement.

'A' registers the posture, the message, as well as the tone and volume of the voice, then closes his eyes.

'B' & 'C' form another posture and add another short statement.

'A' registers the new scenario and then duplicates the first posture and statement of both 'B' & 'C', and then duplicates the second posture and statement of both 'B' & 'C'.

'B' & 'C' give 'A' feedback.

Rotate the roles.

Exercise #10
Modeling A Desired
Physiological State

Purpose: To improve one's flexibility and to further develop sensory acuity.

'B' announces a particular physiological state or desired state he wishes to have 'A' model. (Examples could include happiness, joy, calmness, anger, etc.), but 'B' does not model that state. Instead 'B' maintains his present state.

'B' guides 'A' into his desired state by giving instructions, having 'A' visualize the state, asking questions, etc. The posture, facial expression, and when appropriate, the vocal tone and expression should match 'B's conception of the desired state.

'C' observes and gives feedback.

Sensory feedback will enable 'B' & 'C' to know if 'A' is in the desired state.

Rotate the roles.

Collateral Exercise #10

Purpose: To be able to move students toward states that are conducive to learning.

The teacher selects five students and forms a group. The teacher determines how the group would look and sound if they were in an optimal learning state. The teacher does whatever is necessary to both move the students toward, and to keep them in, this physiological state.

Predicate Patterns & the Classroom

Here is an additional practical suggestion for using predicate patterns in the classroom.

I. Encourage creative writing:

   a. Use a weekly random display of magazine pictures; ask students to choose one, cut and paste it on paper and, then, write several sentences about the picture.

   b. During a given week have students write using predominately visual predicates, another week using predominately auditory predicates and a third week using kinesthetic predicates.

   c. Place an object in front of the class (such as a marshmallow). Have students list words under "sight", "sound", "touch", "smell", and "taste". Students can construct individual stories using the words, or the teacher, using an overhead projector, can develop a group story.

   d. The teacher can correctly write any misspelled theme words in the upper left-hand corner of the student's paper. (The reason for this action is explained in Chapter 4.)

Summary

Before any student can be significantly influenced, it is imperative to first identify the way that student perceives the world. One way this identification can be accomplished is through the process of building rapport by matching predicates and by designing learning activities that match the way the student processes information. Learning to match predicates is a step toward achieving the goal of clear and direct communication.

Chapter 4

ENTRY CUES

The teacher was puzzled. One of his conscientious students who appeared to understand the subject matter, made frequent and intelligent contributions to class discussion and always had his homework finished on time, was not scoring well on his tests. Consequently, the student's grades did not reflect his academic ability. Thinking that test anxiety might be the cause of his low test scores, the teacher was surprised to learn that the student felt very little anxiety when taking tests. Instead, he felt frustrated because he couldn't take his eyes off his paper when he took tests. The student stated that it was easier for him to remember the answers if he was able to look up. Somewhat skeptically, the teacher decided to try an experiment. During the next exam he let this particular student sit in the front row and told him he could look up when he needed to do so. The student followed those directions. To the teacher's amazement the student scored an "A" on this and subsequent exams. Careful observation of his other students indicated to the teacher that when people recall information, their eyes generally shift upward. Realizing that he was penalizing students by forcing them to keep their eyes on their paper when they took tests, the teacher rescinded his rule and was rewarded by his students receiving, as a class, higher test scores!

What are "Entry Cues?" Why are they important in determining the learning patterns of students?

This chapter examines entry cues: involuntary eye movement patterns, breathing patterns, muscle tone and posture changes, vocal tonal and tempo changes, facial skin coloration, and gestures. Each of these cues are indicators of the sensory system(s) that the student is entering to process information internally. This knowledge can prove useful in eliciting and installing learning patterns, which is the subject of Chapter 17.

Eye Movement Patterns

Before you continue reading this chapter, please take the time to do the following practice activity.

Practice Activity E: Determining Eye Movement Patterns

(The following questions prompt the listener to activate specific eye movement patterns.) Ask your friends or family members some of the questions and watch the directions of their eye movements. Determine if there is any similarity between the eye movement patterns of individuals when they are asked the same questions. (You may have to watch the eye movements carefully because some people shift their eyes very quickly or very subtly.)

(1)

When was the last time that you saw the President on TV?

or

Where did you go on your last vacation?

Suppose you were to draw the front of the building in which you live. How would that look?

(2) {

(The last eye shift before the person again looks at you should be the most significant.)

or

How would you look skiing?

(3) {

What is your favorite type of music?

or

Which band instrument sounds most pleasing to you?

(4) {

Your principal has asked you to say a few words to the graduating seniors. Construct what you would say to them.

or

How would it sound if your principal spoke, but Yogi Bear's voice replaced his own?

(5) {

Hear yourself describe to a friend the most exciting time of your life.

or

Listen to yourself give a friend the ingredients of a favorite recipe.

(6) {

How does a fur coat feel?

or

How does the sand on a beach feel?

In the following space, indicate any eye movement similarities or differences between people that you noticed when you asked them the same question(s).

(1)

(2)

(3)

(4)

(5)

(6)

     The purpose of the practice activity was to make you aware that individuals provide cues that indicate at that particular time, which sensory systems are being used. Involuntary eye movement patterns are one such cue. Figure 5 shows visual entry cues for a normally organized right-handed person. V^r indicates visual recall or memory. When remembering something visual, the eyes will shift up and to the observer's right (the subject's left). V^c denotes visual construction or building an image. When constructing an image, the eyes will shift to the viewer's left (the subject's right).

     A^r signifies auditory recall. When remembering something auditory, the eyes will shift horizontally to the viewer's right (the subject's left). A^c conveys auditory construction. When constructing something to say, the eyes shift to the viewer's left (the subject's right). A_d^i designates auditory internal dialogue. An internal conversation will be registered by the eyes shifting to the viewer's lower right hand side (the subject's left).

     K denotes kinesthetic or body sensations. When feeling something, a person's eyes will shift to the viewer's lower left side (the subject's right). A dilation of the pupils and a defocusing of the eyes is a sign that the person is processing internally and is probably visualizing. It should be noted, particularly regarding the auditory shifts, that sometimes the eye movements can occur so rapidly that they are almost imperceptible. The development of more acute observational skills will overcome this difficulty.

     The eye movement patterns are often, but not always, reversed for left-handed people. It is also true that these patterns do not hold true for every right-handed person. However, what will be true is that students who deviate from this pattern will themselves have their own consistent pattern which they will follow. This pattern can be determined through questioning and by observation. Since the highest quality response is always behavioral, a good rule of thumb is to always rely on your sensory observation. If there are any exceptions to the patterns, sensory observation will be able to detect them and the pattern used by the student can then be constructed.

Fig. 5: Eye Entry Cues

(Note: These illustrations show eye movement patterns as they appear when observing a normally organized right-handed student.)

Visual - Constructed Images

(Building An Image)

Visual - Recalled Images

(Remembering An Image)

Auditory - Constructing Words

(Building A Dialogue)

Auditory - Remembering Words

(Remembering A Dialogue)

Kinesthetic

(Internal & External Feeling)

Auditory - Internal Dialogue

(Carrying On An Internal Conversation)

Practice Activity F: This activity will give you practice in determining eye movement patterns. Unless otherwise indicated, assume the individuals are normally organized right-handed people. (The answers will be found in the Appendix on page 226.)

1.   In the spaces below the faces, label the eye movement patterns by placing V^c, V^r, A^c, A^r, A_d^i, or K under each picture.

2.   Match the eye movement pattern with the verbal statement, and in the spaces below the faces, place the appropriate identifying code (V^c, V^r, A^c, A^r, A_d^i, or K).

53

3. Fill in the eyes in the faces below with the appropriate eye movement pattern that best matches the verbal statement. Then, in the spaces below the face, write in the appropriate coding.

4. Assume the individual represented by the drawings below is left-handed and is cerebrally reversed. On the line below the faces write the symbol indicated by the entry cues that best represents the correct eye movement pattern.

Breathing Changes

Breathing is the single most powerful determinate of state! That means that breathing can be correlated to our internal states, both in terms of our feelings and in terms of determining the sensory system in which the student at that moment finds himself. While a certain student's eye movement patterns may not always conform to the Eye Entry Cues Diagram (Fig. 5), <u>breathing changes will remain consistent.</u> Figure 6 is a summary of the findings.

Fig. 6: Breathing Patterns & Sensory Systems

Breathing	Sensory System
In upper chest with little depth.	Visual (V)
Even breathing in mid-chest area.	Auditory (A)
Full breathing in lower stomach area.	Kinesthetic (K)

Teachers having difficulty determining what sensory systems students have entered, would be wise to observe students' breathing patterns. It is the most consistent and accurate method of determining this information.

Posture and Muscle Tone Changes

As students' breathing patterns change to enter a particular sensory system, adjustments are made in their posture and muscle tone to assist entry into that system. Figure 7 describes the changes and gives the sensory systems for them.

Fig. 7: Posture & Muscle Tone Changes & Sensory Systems

Posture & Muscle Tone Changes	Sensory System
Tension in shoulders and neck and sometimes in stomach; shoulders often hunched.	Visual (V)
Tension evenly distributed; shoulders thrown back; head tilted to one side.	Auditory (A)
Muscles relaxed, shoulders drooped; head positioned over shoulders.	Kinesthetic Internal (K^i)
Head and shoulders same as above: body in motion and shoulders held more squarely.	Kinesthetic External (K^e)

Observing posture and muscle tone changes is another method of determining the sensory systems students activate at any given time. This information is best used in conjunction with the breathing patterns information.

Tonal and Tempo Changes

Tonal and tempo changes are closely related to breathing changes and to posture and muscle tone changes, because change in tonality and in voice tempo are caused by changes in breathing and in the muscle tension in the face and neck. Figure 8 illustrates these characteristics.

Tonal & Tempo Changes	Sensory System
Rapid torrent of words in high-pitched nasal or strained tones; rapid tempo.	Visual (V)
Even pace and tempo; midrange pitch; clear tonality; good word enunciation.	Auditory (A)
Slower tempo; longer pauses; lower and deeper pitch.	Kinesthetic (K)

Tonal and tempo changes are helpful aids in identifying the sensory system being utilized by students at that time. The greater linkage that occurs between each of these methods of identifying sensory systems, the more accurate the identification will be. For best results, use this information in conjunction with the other ways to identify sensory systems.

Facial Skin Color

With some light-skinned people, facial color will change as they activate sensory systems. Figure 9 identifies the changes.

Fig. 9: Facial Skin Color & Sensory Systems

Color	Sensory Systems
light flush	Visual (V)
deepening flush	Auditory (A)
deeper flush	Kinesthetic (K)

Facial skin color information should be used in conjunction with the other methods of determining how students process information. Some people will indicate color changes as they activate their sensory systems, but many others will not.

Gestures

People will often use gestures to indicate which particular sensory system is being activated. In fact, they will often touch the part of the body, or organ which illustrates the sensory system. The student who rubs his eyes when you are talking to him, may not be able to "see" your point of view. A student who assumes a position where his tilted head leans on his left hand or fist, is probably involved in an internal auditory dialogue. The student who rubs his stomach after a particularly good lunch is activating his kinesthetic sensory system. Gestures can, of course, occur without the accompanying verbalizations.

Figure 10 summarizes entry cues.

Fig. 10: Entry Cues Summary

Visual	Auditory	Kinesthetic
Eye Movements (From Viewer's Postion)		
Up Left - Visual Construction (V^c).	Horizontal Left - Auditory Construction (A^c).	Down Left (K).
Up Right - Visual Recall (V^r).	Horizontal Right - Auditory Recall (A^r). Down Right - Auditory Internal Dialogue (A^i_d).	
Breathing		
Upper chest with little depth.	Even breathing in mid-chest area.	Full breathing in lower stomach area.
Muscle Tones & Posture		
Tension in shoulder and neck; shoulders often hunched.	Tension evenly distributed; may be slight rhythmic movements; shoulders back; head to one side.	K^i - muscles relaxed head positioned over shoulders; shoulders relaxed, almost droopy. For intense feelings, very deep and full abdominal breathing. K^e - deep and full breathing for intense feelings and in exertion; body in motion & shoulders more squared.
Vocal Tonal & Tempo Changes		
Rapid torrent of words; high pitch; tonality may be nasal or strained; rapid tempo.	Even pace & tempo; midrange pitch; clear tonality; good word enunciation.	Slower tempo, longer pauses; lower, deeper pitch.
Facial Skin Color (When applicable)		
Light in color.	Deepening in color.	Deeper in color.
Other Indicators		
Defocusing of eyes. Dilation of pupils.	Finger or object tapping; clicking; humming or whistling.	

There are correlations between master teacher performances and those of a skilled orchestra conductor. The conductor has a musical score. However, he still must take all the individual musicians with their varied backgrounds and playing abilities and, if necessary, interpret that score to encourage a harmonic blending of sounds. He wants the orchestra's performance to measure up to his artistic interpretation and to do justice to the composition.

The master teacher relies on his observation of his students' sensory feedback to maintain a high degree of student interest in his lesson. He adjusts his lesson when the feedback warrants making an adjustment. The master teacher wants his students' performances to measure up to his goals and to do justice to the subject matter and/or lesson plan.

Exercise #11
A Repeat of Exercise #7

Purpose: To enhance one's auditory and kinesthetic acuity.

Most people find this exercise to be easier when repeated a second time because their auditory-kinesthetic acuity has improved and they have figured out strategies that enable them to make the correct identifications. If you are still having difficulty with this exercise, and your colleagues are more successful in identifying the combinations, ask them how they are obtaining the correct answers. Then try that strategy or modify your own to see if you can improve your success rate.

'A' closes his eyes.

'B' makes a sound, then touches 'A' and identifies self.

'C' does the same.

'A' calibrates the sounds and touches with each persons, then 'A' is to guess whether 'B' or 'C' has made the sounds and done the touching. 'B' and 'C' should first make obvious sounds and movements, but should make them more subtle as the exercise progresses.

After 'A' has identified the combinations correctly for four or five times consecutively, then 'B' and 'C' can mix the sounds and touches, and 'A' can then identify who has made the sound and who has done the touching.

Rotate the roles.

Collateral Exercise #11
Repeat of #7

Purpose: To transfer one's auditory and kinesthetic acuity to the classroom.

The teacher selects several students who in turn select an object symbolizing themselves. The teacher either closes his eyes or is blindfolded. The students agree on a word or tone among themselves. Each student, one at a time, makes the tone or says the word, hands the object to the teacher, and identifies himself.

The teacher calibrates to these students and identifies the students four or five times consecutively.

To make the exercise more challenging, the students mix the sounds and the objects and the teacher identifies the student who has made the sound and the one who handed the object to the teacher.

Exercise #12
Auditory Discovery

Purpose: To improve flexibility and auditory acuity.

'A' states a sentence.

'B' repeats the sentence utilizing the tone, tempo, timbre, quality, intonation of 'A'.

'C' observes and indicates when 'B' has successfully reproduced 'A's sentence. 'C' may coach when necessary.

'A' does a total of 3 sentences, one at a time. 'B' matches each sentence.

Rotate the roles.

Collateral Exercise #12

Purpose: To practice auditory acuity in the classroom.

The teacher subtly matches the tone, tempo, timbre and intonation of the comments of several students.

The teacher could tape a class and then analyze the tape to see how closely he matched the students' vocal tone, tempo, timber and intonation.

Exercise #13 - Visual Auditory
& Kinesthetic Discovery

Purpose: To heighten one's sensory acuity and ability to mirror an individual.

'A' selects one of his beliefs and states 20 seconds of that belief.

'B' observes 'A's sensory output and mirrors 'A's movements or gestures (including facial expressions), and repeats 'A's key words.

'C' observes and gives 'B' feedback and coaching, if necessary.

Rotate the roles.

Collateral Exercise #13

Purpose: To transfer the ability to mirror a person to the classroom.

The teacher selects a group of five students. Each student discusses for several minutes an idea for which he has strong feelings.

The teacher responds to each student immediately after the student finishes his discussion, by mirroring several of the student's gestures and by repeating key words of the student.

The teacher carefully observes each student's reactions to his feedback.

Eye Movement Patterns and The Classroom

Here are some practical applications for using eye entry cues in the classroom.

1. When learning student's names, place the name tag in the upper left-handed corner of the desk (assuming the teacher is a normally-organized right-handed person). This action places the name in the teacher's V^r area.

2. Keep an information card file on students. Such information as the student's name and the sensory system predominately utilized by the student, along with the student's significant learning patterns and other pertinent information could be placed in the upper left hand corner of the card (V^r). The eye entry modalities of the student could also be drawn on the card. These modalities could be determined in a beginning-of-school interview.

3. Bulletin boards could reflect the eye entry cues by placing material to be remembered in the upper left-hand corner, imaginary or constructed directions or materials in the upper right-hand corner, kinesthetically oriented material in the lower right-hand corner (this could include projects, etc.), and by placing other directions to correspond to auditory eye entry material.

4. Use color coding to indicate the differences between beginning consonants, blends and vowel sounds.

<u>b</u> o o k, <u>b</u> a g, <u>b</u> a t, <u>c</u> a t, etc.

5. When possible, construct worksheet designs to match eye movement patterns.

6. Each week's spelling words could be hung in the upper left-hand corner of the classroom.

7. Use flash cards. Hold the flash card high on the right-hand side; instruct the student to look at the flash card, to take a picture of it, and to look away. Then ask the student to tell you the information. Ask him to write it in the air with his finger. Then, ask the student to write the material either on his paper or on the blackboard.

Summary

The sensory systems of students can be determined by observing entry cues (eye movement patterns, breathing patterns, posture and muscle tone changes, vocal and tempo changes, and gestures). Perhaps, the two cues most easily observed and learned are eye movement patterns and breathing patterns. Of those two patterns, breathing patterns will best indicate the sensory system being entered. Since learning patterns are but a series of sensory systems linked together, knowing how to determine sensory systems will pave the way for knowing how to elicit and to install learning patterns.

Chapter 5

THE BRAIN

The Master paused to reflect on the state of the art of teaching. He reflected on his early teaching experience where students had been "lumped" into specific categories allegedly according to their learning abilities. He remembered how he accidentally discovered that a group of "slow" learners were very adept at building a model of an Indian village and that they excelled at kinesthetic activities. He remembered his own inexperience and inflexibility for not designing similar kinds of learning activities that would have enabled those students to have been more successful learners.

The Master reflected on the many different learning styles he had observed his students using and how his early teaching methods, which were his best efforts at that time, in retrospect now looked futile and incompetent. He remembered his concern for those bright students who were unable to break their bonds and rise to their potential and how frustrated he had been when his efforts to assist them failed. These early experiences were valuable because they taught him to always be alert for new teaching methods and training programs that would help him better meet the needs of his students. He marveled at the flow of new information about the brain and learning styles, and how much of this information confirmed what he had intuitively known and had sought to accomplish in his teaching career.

The Master recalled with considerable satisfaction the progress that he had made since his early teaching career. While his title of "Master" had been earned and was well deserved, he realized that learning is a life-long process and that a true "Master" seeks more effective methods of sharing his experiences and skills with his students. It was not a time to become complacent; instead it was a time to again become a "seeker."

What, specifically, are the functions of each brain hemisphere? What implications do these functions have for teachers? How does McCarthy classify "learning styles"? How can these findings be combined with Master Teaching Techniques?

In the 1960's Dr. Roger Sperry began to practice split brain surgery techniques to alleviate severe epileptic seizures in selected patients. In this procedure the corpus callosum, the 200 million nerve fibers connecting the left and right brain hemispheres, are severed. Consequently, the epileptic seizures are limited to one hemisphere, leaving a second hemisphere to function undisturbed, and the patient is able to function more normally. As a result of the surgery, the normal transmissions that integrate the two hemispheres cease. However, the lack of communication between the two hemispheres does not affect the normal daily experiences of the patient, because both hemispheres receive the same information. For the first time, it now became possible to feed information to a single hemisphere and to determine if there were any differences in the way each hemisphere functioned. From a small number of such cases, generalizations were made that the left hemisphere tends to be linear, sequential, structural, and verbal, and that it controls speech, computes mathematical functions and organizes and categorizes. It was also generalized that the right hemisphere controls the non-verbal, that it experiences life in a visual and spatial context, that it is more spontaneous and arrives at decisions intuitively, that it tends to be musical, sexual, emotional and holistic, (adept at visualizing whole patterns).[2] Thus the hemispheres were supposed to have both specialized skills and distinctive cognitive styles.

---

[2]For some people, especially left-handed people, these functions may be reversed.

There is now considerable controversy over the accuracy of these generalizations. Two of the leaders in testing split brain patients, Dr. Jerre Levy and Dr Michael Gazzaniga, have had major disagreements over the information resulting from those tests. Levy, whom Sperry sides with, believes that the right brain is specialized for holistic processes and that the left brain is necessary for analytical purposes. Gazzaniga, in his book, The Social Brain, contends that the data is too limited for such generalizations, and that what is important is not where things are located, but that specific tasks are handled by specific brain systems. He proposes a modular brain theory, which states that the brain is a vast confederacy of hundreds or thousands of independent modules. These modules process information from a person's internal and external environment, and each module activates its own thoughts and actions. The modules express themselves by stimulating us to engage in a certain behavior, or by communicating to the module responsible for our ability to verbalize, and the information is then expressed verbally. He further states that the brain also has a module, separate from the speech module, and probably located in the left hemisphere, that acts as an "interpreter" - it constructs theories as to why we do certain things.

Furthermore, Gazzaniga states that visual imagery is separate from our visual system and that mental images are created in a module located in the left hemisphere. This contradicts the popular theory that visualization is a right hemisphere process.

What is thought of as our "unconscious" mind, he theorizes, is actually composed of modules that are conscious, but are non-verbal. Their inability to communicate directly with the verbal module, does not mean that these modules are "unconscious". This idea could explain our intuitive abilities.

Gazzaniga's ideas also help explain why the Transforming process described in Chapter 17 works.

If Gazzaniga's theory turns out to be accurate, the idea of a person being right-brained, or left-brained makes little sense. It may be that the brain structure of some people causes them to rely more on their non-verbal module. (We have referred to these people as being "right-brained" in the past.) Since most schools have traditionally used such teaching techniques, as lecture, which appeals to the student whose brain structure allows easier access to verbal modules, (formerly "left-brained" students), the needs of the student who processes through his non-verbal modules have been ignored. There is a need for educators to teach in ways that will reach both types of students. The educational experience and/or learning will also be more fully integrated and therefore, learned and retained. (For ease of understanding, the remainder of this chapter uses the terms "left-brained" and "right-brained".)

To carry this idea further, more educators are now exploring learning style differences. Some of us prefer to learn by visual means, (through pictures, visual demonstration and by making and using mental images), others prefer to learn predominantly by auditory means, (listening to words or sounds and through the use of internal dialogue), while others prefer to learn predominately by kinesthetic means, (through feelings or body movement). Some people learn best in groups; others learn best individually. Some people learn best in the morning, while others learn better in the afternoon. Educators need to be able to vary their teaching styles, because with all of the variables that operate in an educational environment, there is not one educational teaching method that best meets everyone's learning style.

Learning style characteristics and ways to teach those learning styles are discussed by Bernice McCarthy in an excellent book entitled The 4Mat System.

McCarthy classifies the "Type One" learner as an "innovative learner." Innovative learners are interested in personal meaning. They learn by watching, sensing, and feeling. They tend to be "idea" people, and have plenty of innovation and imagination. Type One learners need to be given reasons why they have to study a particular unit or activity.

McCarthy classifies "Type Two" learners as "analytic." Analytic learners love facts and enjoy forming models and concepts. Analytic learners rely heavily on learning by reflecting upon ideas. In comparison with Type One learners, analytic learners seek the facts of the situation, rather than the reasons for studying the material.

"Type Three" learners, McCarthy categorizes as "common-sense learners." Their learning style makes use of concrete experiences, with emphasis on how something works. Abstract ideas are of little interest to this group of learners; their overriding need is to know the way school will help them function better in "real life." The common-sense learner draws inferences through kinesthetic experiences.

McCarthy classifies the "Type Four" learner as a "dynamic learner." Dynamic learners learn through the process of self-discovery. They seek to determine what can be developed from concepts and ideas. They adapt well to change, even seeking it, and they tend to be flexible in their relationships with others. Dynamic learners learn concretely and seek to process their learnings in an active way.

Three major points that McCarthy seeks to make about learning styles are:

1. All learning styles are of equal importance.

2. Since what both hemispheres of the brain have to offer is useful, teachers should seek to holistically integrate the two halves of the brain through their teaching methods.

3. Through her experiences, her reading, and her research, McCarthy found that by far the largest percentage of students had right brain dominance. Teachers, however, with their emphasis on the cognitive aspects of education, primarily instruct for the left hemisphere. McCarthy believes that teachers need to adapt their teaching styles to reach all four learning styles. She believes that this adaptation can be effectively accomplished by using right and left mode teaching techniques.

Three of the four types of learners identified by McCarthy are right-brain oriented. "Type One," the "innovative" learner, is imaginative and seeks personal meaning in his work. "Type Three," the "common-sense" learner seeks concrete experiences that will aid him in real life. "Type Four," the "dynamic" learner prefers learning via self-discovery through concrete experiences. Although currently there is no research which supports this idea, observation indicates that these three types of learners prefer to process and to learn information through visual and particularly in the case of "Type Three", kinesthetic means.

McCarthy's "Type Two," or "analytic" learner is fact-oriented and prefers to develop models and concepts. The "Type Two" learner is left-brain oriented and therefore, finds it easier to be logical and verbal. Learning information for this student will probably be easier using visual and auditory means.

Although too new to be extensively researched, McCarthy's learning style ideas hold promise because they attempt to meet the needs of each type of learner, one-quarter of the time. The 4Mat System also teaches both right and left-brained activities for each type of learner. Another advantage of her ideas are that no special instrument is necessary to identify the students.

Teachers would find a fertile field in eliciting learning patterns from each student type and installing them in students needing or desiring such patterns (see Chapter 17). With the "analytic" learner, install creative, holistic or intuitive patterns. With the right hemisphere oriented student, install logical, analytic and linear patterns. A case in point centered around two such students. One student was fact-oriented, logical (a typical left hemisphere analytic student) and had a high grade-point average. When it came to artistic activities, he was unable to match his normal achievement. The second student (a typical right hemisphere oriented individual), was exceptionally creative in work, in music and in the theatre. In those subjects reflecting the creative areas, she did exceptionally well and received high grades; in the more analytical and logical subjects, she did poorly. The teacher elicited the learning pattern which served the analytical person well and installed it in the creative student. The teacher then elicited the learning pattern from the creative student and installed it in the analytical student. The results were impressive! The new learning patterns enabled each student to realize their existing resources, talents and potential. The analytical student became more creative without losing any of his logical abilities, and the creative student was better able to use logic when it was necessary, without any loss of her creative abilities.

Exercise #14
Individual Sensory Acuity Drill

Purpose: To heighten sensory acuity.

The teacher focuses his attention and:

Locates five separate images through his peripheral vision.

Identifies five separate sounds.

Is aware of five physical sensations.

Discuss with your group what you noticed each time about your acuity.

Exercise #15
Flexibility Drill
(2 or 3 People)

Purpose: To enhance flexibility.

'A' projects a chosen behavioral state such as depression, disinterest, hurt, haughtiness, bewilderment, etc., without orally describing it.

'B' attempts to correctly identify the state.

'A' coaches 'B' nonverbally if 'B' has difficulty identifying the state; if necessary 'A' projects the same state differently so 'B' can correctly identify the state.

'C' observes.

Rotate the roles.

Exercise #16
Three-State Identification

Purpose: To learn to identify states.

'C' turns away from 'A' and 'B'.

'A' models three different internal experiences and indicates to 'B' when he accesses each experience.

'B' mirrors the three experiences of 'A', to 'C'.

(Continued)

Collateral Exercise #14

Purpose: To transfer one's heightened sensory acuity to the classroom.

The teacher focuses his attention in his classroom and:

Locates five separate images through his peripheral vision

Identifies five separate sounds.

Is aware of five physical sensations.

Collateral Exercise #15

Purpose: To enhance flexibility in the classroom.

The teacher selects five students and identifies some of their major state changes either throughout a period or throughout a day.

To verify that their state change and the teacher's perceptions of that state change are accurate, the teacher feeds back a verbal statement to the student, such as: "You look like you're only mildly interested in this project." The student will either verify the statement or deny it.

Collateral Exercise #16

Purpose: To identify states in the classroom.

The teacher selects several students. The teacher observes the students, makes mental snapshots of the students when they are in states of interest and states of disinterest. Differences such as posture, gestures, eye movement patterns, breathing, and vocal tone and tempo are compared.

'B' repeats the experiences a second time.

'C' then duplicates the experiences and mixes up the order.

'B' identifies the order of the experiences.

Rotate the roles.

Summary

"Controversial," is the word best describing what is known regarding the specialized skills and cognitive functions of the brain hemispheres. Beginning in the 1960's, Dr. Roger Sperry performed split-brain operations on patients to alleviate their epileptic seizures. Tests were performed on these patients by Gazzaniga, Levy, and others. Using these test results, which represented a limited number of studies, people outside the field made generalizations regarding the specific skills and cognitive functions of each hemisphere.

Many of these generalizations have been rejected by Gazzaniga and Levy. Gazzaniga has since rejected Levy and Sperry's ideas that the left brain is necessary for analytical purposes and that the right brain is specialized for holistic processes. His modular theory of the brain opens up a whole new vista for explaining the functions of the brain.

McCarthy has identified four types of learners: innovative, analytic, common-sense and dynamic. Her research has indicated that most students are right-brain oriented. She believes that teachers need to change their teaching strategies to reach all of the four types of learners. Master Teaching Techniques provides a structure and techniques to identify the types of learning activities (visual, auditory, and kinesthetic) from which each type of student would benefit. The elicitation of learning patterns such as a creativity pattern from right-brain oriented student types, and logical, analytical patterns from the left-brain oriented student types, and the installation of the right-brain pattern in the left-brain student and vice versa, could prove to be a major factor that would enable students to function fully as human beings.

Chapter 6

SUMMARY AND NEW BEGINNINGS

Uncle Remus's Br'er Rabbit was frequently involved in some interesting predicaments. Br'er Fox and Br'er Bear were continually trying to catch Br'er Rabbit and Br'er Rabbit was continually trying to outwit them. One day Br'er Fox and Br'er Bear decided to see if they could outwit that pesky rabbit and catch him. To do this they made a baby out of tar, put a hat and shirt on it, and placed it in the road where they knew Br'er Rabbit was certain to come hopping along. Sure enough, along he came. He cordially said, "Hello!" to the tar baby and of course received no response. This lack of response perturbed Br'er Rabbit and after several more attempts to get a suitable response from the tar baby, he became angry, threatened to punch the tar baby and finally "let fly." "Plop!" One paw was now a prisoner of the tar baby. Br'er Rabbit hollered and told the tar baby to let go or he would hit him with the other paw. No response. "Blip!" Now another paw was stuck. Br'er Rabbit threatened to kick the tar baby. "Blam, Blam!" Now all of Br'er Rabbit's paws were firmly stuck. Br'er Fox and Br'er Bear had observed the entire spectacle from a vantage point where they couldn't be seen and heard, and were now clutching their sides and rolling on the ground in shrieks of laughter. One possible moral of this fable is that: RIGID RESPONSES TO STICKY SITUATIONS FREQUENTLY LEAD TO FURTHER ENTANGLEMENTS!

Many teachers may be using some of the ideas discussed in this book without being aware of it. However, by consciously learning and practicing all of the ideas and techniques, integration of the techniques will occur unconsciously. This integration will result in a more consistent, high-quality teaching performance and will offer "disentanglement" from sticky classroom situations.

Section I emphasized that for effective learning to occur, teaching methods should address both sides of the brain. Sensory systems were explained, and the idea of the sensory set (V, A, K & O) was introduced. Because each person perceives the world differently, each student has his own perception or model of the world. An awareness of the important aspects comprising each person's model and the ability to reach that person's model are the basics of successful teaching.

Most students tend to use particular predicate patterns at a given moment. From these patterns and from the entry cues used by a student, (eye movement patterns, breathing changes, posture and muscle tone changes, vocal tonal and tempo changes, facial skin colorations and gestures), the student's dominant sensory system and his learning patterns can be determined. The significance of this information will be apparent as Section II unfolds.

SECTION TWO

The Structure of Effective Teaching

Chapter 7

OVERVIEW OF SECTION II

The debate had generated more "heat than light!" Each side was sincere, well-intentioned and thought that it had the "truth." The subject matter specialists knew that unless their students learned what they taught they would not be well-rounded individuals, life would be less meaningful for them and that what society considered "progress" would decrease. To these specialists, students needed to be told what they should know. The lecture method was an appropriate tool that had existed for hundreds of years, and while it might require some occasional modification it still was a superior way of conveying information to students.

The educational methodologists acknowledged the importance of learning subject matter but insisted that because students learned in different ways, different methods of subject matter presentation were needed. The lecture method was good in some instances, but since students learned in a variety of ways, it could not meet the needs of all students.

During the debate the Master, with inward amusement, quietly listened to the argument of each side but made no comment. The debators, realizing that no agreement would be reached between them, turned to the Master to seek approval for their arguments. As was frequently his manner, the Master appeared to agree with both sides while introducing a different and generally more profound idea. "Rather than being concerned about subject matter as an end in itself, or about the various ways to present subject matter, would it not be wise to teach students learning patterns that would teach them how to learn? In this way students could apply what they considered to be significant learnings to their own lives for the betterment of themselves and of society."

What information is covered in this section? What is "teaching?" What techniques and areas of expertise are part of the teaching process?

Section II shows many ways to improve teaching skills and to bring about changes in student behavior. Specific techniques are taught in this section for these six purposes:

> **Building rapport**
>
> **Calibrating eye movement patterns**
>
> **Assisting students in identifying outcomes**
>
> **Helping students draw on their own resources to change their behavior**
>
> **Gathering needed information**
>
> **Keeping information relevant.**

The "when" and "how to" of Remedial and Developmental change techniques are fully explained in this section. The Teacher Intervention Structured Overview (Fig. 12) has been developed to serve as a structured overview for this section.

Sensory exercises and collateral exercises accompany most of the chapters in this section. Section II takes the important information discussed in the first portion of this book and shows how it can be applied to make teaching experiences truly memorable!

Teaching

The word "teaching" implies that it is possible to present knowledge or skills in a way that the learner will understand the knowledge, and in certain situations, will be able to execute selected skills.

Why some teachers are more successful in achieving their instructional goals than are others has been a concern of teacher educators for decades. Most teacher educators believe that it is possible for both prospective and experienced teachers to change their behavior and move toward the goal of being more effective teachers. Individuals become effective teachers for a number of reasons. They may have had good models to emulate, or they may have had exceptional methods teachers, or they may have had experiences which made them good teachers, or a combination of these and other factors.

In this book, successful teaching means that teachers are able to keep students in physiological states that indicate receptivity to learning so that the teachers' instructional goals will be met. It also means that individual student outcomes are realized. Effective teaching requires not only the knowledge of the elements in the "teaching wheel" (Fig. 11), but the ability and the skills to incorporate them into the classroom environment so that the instructional goals and individual student outcomes become achieveable.

Master teachers, although they may not always be consciously aware that they use the traits in the wheel, continually do make use of them. With the possible exception of the concepts of brain hemisphere differences, language patterns, establishment of rapport, and individual learning pattern sequences, the ideas in the wheel are covered in most textbooks. These "exceptions" have either already been discussed in Section I of this book, or will be discussed in this section.

Fig. 11: The Teaching Process

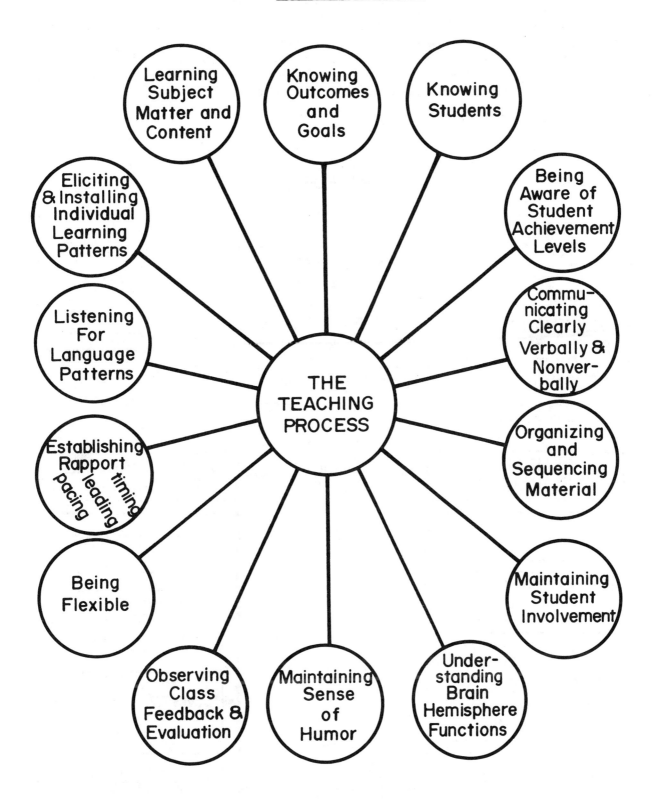

Fig. 12: <u>The Teacher Intervention Structured Overview</u>

The purpose of the Teacher Intervention Structured Overview is to serve as a visual guide to Section II. Beginning with Chapter 9 and ending with Chapter 17, each chapter "chunks down" and explains a portion of Figure 12. By thoroughly understanding and experiencing each chapter, the reader can "chunk up" and will be ready to use one or more of the intervention techniques when they are needed.

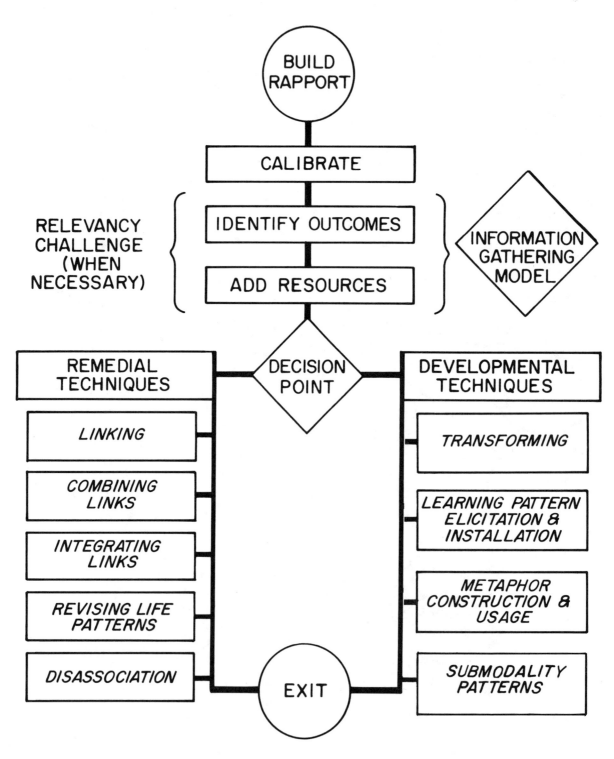

SUMMARY

The "Teaching Wheel" illustrates the many areas of expertise needed by teachers to be successful. The new and unfamiliar areas illustrated in the "Teaching Wheel" are dealt with in Section II and will give teachers new and valuable tools and techniques to improve teaching performance.

After reading and underlinedexperiencing the material in this section, it is possible that teaching may never again be the same for any of you!

Chapter 8

THE PRINCIPLES OF LEARNING REVISITED

There was once a renowned cultural anthropologist. Every summer he took a group of his students on an ocean voyage to study the culture of some Pacific Island natives. The trips were safe, popular, and the students found them interesting. However one summer, miles from any land, the boat caught fire and burned. The anthropologist and his students managed to leave the boat with two dinghies, some navigational maps and enough food and water to last several days. The information that they had last received from their navigator indicated that land was about a three day journey from the point that their boat went down. For several days they alternately rowed and rested in the blazing sun and in the cool nights. On noon of the fourth day the burned, thirsty and hungry group spied an island. Everyone screamed for joy except the anthropologist. He knew that the island was an illusion, a mirage. As any good professor would (or should), he presented the bad news as facts to his students. They refused to accept his "facts" because the students knew what they were seeing was real. A great argument ensued. The anthropologist could not convince the students that the island was really a mirage, so he allowed them to take one boat and go to the mirage, while he took the other boat and continued to seek help. The anthropologist had figured their approximate location on a map, and the students agreed that if they discovered a mirage instead of an island they would drop a sea anchor and wait for the help that the professor was certain he would find.

The students rowed off toward their island and the professor continued on. Hours later, to the joy of the students, they found an island with fresh water, fruit, friendly natives and a radio. The students sought help for their professor, but he was never found again.

How do the "Principles of Learning" relate to teaching?

In the portion of this book entitled, ABOUT THIS BOOK, a number of basic "Principles of Learning" were listed. These "Principles" served as a basis for the material to be presented in subsequent chapters in Section I. These "Principles of Learning" have a tremendous impact on the teaching process from both the perspectives of the student and of the teacher. The "Principles" have been slightly rewritten from the way they were presented in Section I, to emphasize their relationship to the teaching process.

Principle #1: Teachers need to establish desired states based on physiological feedback from their students.

When students are actively involved in the learning process, they exhibit non-verbal signals through their posture, facial expressions, eye movement patterns, breathing patterns, voice tone, tempo, gestures, etc. Teachers should develop a visual image of what student behavior constitutes a desired learning state for their particular learning situation. With that state in mind, the teacher has a target to work toward. The teacher can engage in state-change activities, or he can use specific methods to move the students toward the desired state and keep them there. The students' sensory feedback will always serve as a barometer of the teacher's success in keeping students in states conducive to learning. The longer a teacher is able to keep students in the desired state, the greater the possiblity will be for successful teaching-learning experiences to occur. The feedback you see from your students is not a mirage -- use it!

Principle #2: The person having the most flexibility in the teaching-learning relationship will maintain control.

The teacher using one primary technique day after day will probably have bored students on his hands. Bored students either tune completely out or find ways to relieve their boredom, usually at the expense of the teacher and the teacher's instructional goals. The strategies that teachers utilize must of necessity be geared toward teacher goals, but those strategies must also take into account student needs. The master teacher has many strategies to choose from and will employ as many as are needed to effectively reach his students.

Students also have a number of strategies to use to reach their goals. Like teachers, students find that some of their strategies are ineffective and/or innappropriate for some learning situations. Successful students will have a variety of strategies from which to draw. Conversely, less successful teachers and students will have fewer strategies and options. If a teacher's methodology is not making use of all of the sensory systems, then he probably is not effectively teaching all of his students. Teachers need to include all sensory systems in their teaching methodology. Therefore, if what you are doing is not achieving your teaching goals, change what you are doing.

The following statement is an extension of this second "Principle." **Students' resistance to teacher communication is indicative of teacher inflexibility.** Simply stated, students' resistance can be overcome with more skillful teaching techniques. To illustrate, if students show resistance during a lesson, the teacher can change students' states by engaging in whatever communication seems appropriate and effective in moving those students toward the desired learning state selected by the teacher.

Principle #3: There is no substitute for the development of the ability to observe rapid and minute behavioral changes in students.

Sharpening sensory acuity requires practice. The ability to observe sensory changes such as eye entry cues, give excellent feedback regarding each student's progress toward the desired state. Sensory acuity is also indispensable in identifying students' learning patterns. For example, if a teacher wanted to have students access subject matter visually, the lesson could be structured by asking questions or making statements that would force the students to access visually. "Imagine what it would have looked like building the Trojan Horse. Watch it being constructed. Can you see the men climb inside the horse? Watch it as it is being rolled outside the city gates. Now draw a picture of what you think the horse would have looked like as it stood outside the gates of Troy." The students' eye movements could then be observed to determine if they were visualizing. If observation of the students' breathing patterns indicated that breathing was centered in their upper chests, this fact would also verify that visualization was taking place.

Principle #4: **Regardless of how inappropriate, bizarre, or malicious a student's behavior may appear, sound or feel, that behavior is the best choice at that point in time for that student.**

Students' undesirable behavior indicates a lack of flexibility on the part of those particular students. For example, a student's behavior indicates frustration in completing math problems. If an elicitation of the student's math learning pattern indicates that the learning pattern is a poor one, the teacher could alter the learning pattern sequence which would have the effect of giving the student an increased opportunity to make another choice, a choice which would have a positive effect on his learning and on his feelings.

Summary

These "Principles" are vital aspects of the teaching and learning process. Maintaining flexibility allows one to gain and/or maintain control. In the anthropologist's case, had he been flexible enough to trust what he saw, he would have been saved.

Improving sensory acuity allows the teacher to gather important information about students' progress. Since effective communication is determined by the response the communicator gets, each teacher is responsible for the outcome of his communication. Students make the best response that they can at that particular time. Teacher flexibility can overcome students' resistance. Applying the information provided by the Principles will make teaching more challenging (by determining how to integrate the Principles into existing teaching methodology), interesting (by observing, listening to, and feeling the changes that occur), and effective (by being able to evoke desired responses from students).

Chapter 9

ESTABLISHING RAPPORT

In many situations I have intuitively established rapport with people. One situation that I particularly remember occurred when I had to fill in for my department chairperson at an educational meeting. This group of state educators met twice a year and had been meeting over a period of several years. I was a total stranger to the other participants, but by the end of three hours one of the participants remarked to me, "I feel like I've known you three months instead of three hours." I appreciated the comment but at the time I gave it little thought. As I now analyze my actions, one thing that I did was to make conscious efforts to get to know many of the participants. I showed an interest in them by asking questions about themselves and about their jobs. I also matched the content of their conversation and, in all probability, I unconsciously matched the posture, gestures and possibly the vocal tone and tempo of many of the people with whom I talked. These actions enabled me to relate to their model of the world and to establish an intense rapport with them. As a result, my effectiveness as a college representative was greatly enhanced.

What is "Rapport?" Why is it necessary for teachers to establish "rapport" with their students? How can intense personal rapport be established with students? What do the terms "pacing" and "leading" mean?

Simply defined, rapport is a state in which a person is most responsive to us. The establishment of rapport is an important and necessary cornerstone for the development of good communication. The master teacher establishes good rapport with his students because he realizes that students will learn more easily if the student-teacher relationship is a positive one. Rapport is generally established on the unconscious level. Teachers who automatically establish good rapport would probably not even be able to describe the process they use to establish rapport. However, rapport can be established through conscious, scientific techniques. A conscientious examination of these rapport-building techniques will allow a modification, a reconstruction, or an addition to the existing techniques that teachers already use. Further practice will lead to an unconscious integration of the skills.

Establishing rapport begins with well developed sensory acuity. The establishment of rapport depends upon teachers observing changes in sensory activity and responding appropriately. Likewise, being aware of the major sensory systems (V, A & K), the

---

* denotes the part of Fig. 12 being discussed.

predicate patterns of students and the entry cues that they use, and then adjusting one's own response, are prerequisites for rapport development.

Pacing

Pacing allows the teacher to make contact with the students' model of the world and to establish a conscious and unconscious rapport with students. Pacing includes:

Matching predicates and/or voice tone, volume and tempo

Mirroring techniques

Switching

Leading.

The idea of matching predicates has already been discussed. Predicate usage will indicate to teachers whether V, A or K activities are most appropriate to teach selected students. Matching predicates is also one way to establish rapport. Matching or mirroring the voice tone, volume and tempo of students is also an effective way to establish rapport. Another option is to match the content of students' conversations or discussions.

Using mirroring techniques to establish rapport involves subtly matching one or more of the following: eye movement pattern, facial expression, gesture, and posture. If students realize that in some way you are using mirroring techniques on them, and they call attention to that fact, it is helpful to have a ready response that can be used as a retort: "I was so interested in what you were saying, I was not even aware I was doing that."

"Switching" means that the teacher matches one sensory system by shifting into another to accomplish the mirroring. An example of this type of indirect mirroring would be to pace the tempo of students' voices (an auditory representation), by moving a finger, a pencil, or nodding the head (visual representation) while maintaining the same tempo. Another example of "switching" would be to match students' breathing (a kinesthetic representation), by tapping a toe, flicking a foot, moving a hand (visual representations), or by using voice tempo (an auditory representation).

The object of pacing is to establish rapport with students. To determine if rapport has been successfully established, the teacher makes a subtle change in his behavior. This change is called "leading." If a teacher is matching predicates, then an example of "leading" in that context would be to introduce predicates of a different sensory system. If students also start using predicates from the new sensory system, then the teacher would know that he had established rapport. The same would be true for the teacher matching voice tone, tempo or pitch. An altering of any of the three and a duplication of that alteration by students would indicate an establishment of rapport.

If students fail to follow the teacher's lead, the teacher has several options. He can attempt to again establish rapport matching the same sensory system in the same manner for a longer period of time before he tries leading, he may wish to mirror and lead another sensory system, or he may wish to utilize switching. The point to remember is that after a reasonable amount of time has been spent using a mirroring technique and the attempt at leading does not work, do something else such as matching another sensory system.

The same process occurs in switching. A teacher paces students' breathing by slightly moving the index finger every time students' breathe. To check for rapport, the teacher leads by moving his finger in a slightly faster rhythm (if the breathing has been slow and deep), or more slowly if the breathing has been rapid and shallow. If students respond to the subtle change, rapport has been established.

For example, a teacher wants to assist a student who is having difficulty learning a particular subject. A conference is scheduled, or time is taken out of class period while other students are working, to discuss the problem. The teacher's first goal is to establish rapport. The teacher has the option of using one or several or all of the pacing maneuvers. Usually, one or two pacing techniques will suffice and the teacher can then lead to see if rapport has been established. For the purposes of this example, illustrations of each type of pacing will be given. The teacher chooses to make some general conversation regarding his concern about the student's progress. As a first step in gaining rapport, he decides to match the student's breathing rate by using a switching technique of nodding his head in rhythm with the student's breathing. (It is generally recommended that breathing is best paced by using a switching technique because matching students' breathing rates can result in the teacher taking on students' states.) After a couple of minutes of pacing the breathing, the teacher may choose to lead the student by changing the rhythm of his head nods to determine if rapport has been established. Another choice would be to establish further rapport by matching the student's posture. (Leading can be tried any time after the teacher thinks rapport has been established.) The teacher decides to match the student's predicates. The student says, "I just can't see how to do it! I keep looking at it, but it doesn't make sense." Since the predicates are visual, the teacher feeds back visual predicates, "What would help you to get a clear picture of how to complete this work?", or "What would you need to see in order to know how to proceed?" The teacher also uses hand movements to direct the student's eyes toward the appropriate eye movement pattern. Assuming a normally organized right-handed student, the teacher's hand movement would move to the student's upper right (V^c). (The hand movement encourages the student to move his eyes toward the visual construction attitude. This movement can help the student to better "see" how to complete his work.) Additional feedback or predicates could follow.

The student might use predicates from the other sensory systems in some kind of sequence. "I can't see how to do this, even though I listen carefully to your explanation. I just can't get a handle on things." The teacher can decide to match the tone, tempo and pitch of the student's voice, or to match the student's facial expressions, or to match the more obvious gestures. The teacher can lead at any time, by changing whatever he is matching or pacing. If the student follows the teacher's lead, then a particularly high level of rapport has been established. If the student does not follow the teacher's lead, then the pacing should be continued either following the original plan, or the teacher can try a different pacing technique. Teachers interested in establishing a powerful rapport with a particular student can move from a superficial to a deeper rapport by first matching the student's posture, then matching his voice, then his predicate patterns, and then his breathing (via switching).

A skilled person can establish rapport in anywhere from thirty seconds to five minutes. Remember to continually maintain rapport. Periodic leading will indicate whether rapport is being maintained.

Pacing A Class Or A Group

The teacher can pace individual students within a class by matching their predicates, voice tones, tempos and pitches. When students ask questions and use gestures, the teacher can pace students by matching their gestures when answering questions. When appropriate, the teacher can also use hand gestures to direct eye movements to provide entry to the various major sensory systems (V, A & K).

The teacher can assume a particular body posture and/or series of gestures when he wishes the group to enter a particular sensory system. Each time students use predicates of a particular sensory system, the teacher can assume the body posture and make the gestures that correspond to that sensory system. In this way the students are also being paced. Likewise the voice tones, tempos and pitches can be used in a similar manner. (When used in this manner, the postures, gestures, voice tones, tempos and volumes are known as "links" because they are stimuli that provide "links" to certain responses.)

By paying attention to the sensory systems of individual students, the teacher can pace students by offering activities geared toward that sensory system or the teacher can ask questions or make comments in class that match the sensory systems of selected students. (Since our culture tends to favor a visual processing of information, teachers should pace their students' visual modality by offering more information visually, instead of relying so heavily on auditory presentations.)

Teachers can track groups in a number of ways. One technique is to pace a class in terms of their voice level, their tone, their movements and postures and their conversational content. Once rapport has been established, the teacher can lead by bringing his voice to his typical teaching voice and his posture to his typical teaching posture.

Group leaders can be paced and led to more easily control the class. Aspects of the behavior of group leaders can be modeled by the teacher allowing the teacher to maintain control of the group, but still allowing the group leader to function.

Pacing and leading are always easier to do when the subject is not aware of your intention. Nevertheless, pacing and leading are possible even when the subject is aware that establishing rapport is your outcome. You may wish to try the following exercises with your group. I encourage you to experiment with pacing and leading in less contrived situations.

Exercise #17
Establishing Rapport

Purpose: To learn to establish rapport by matching body position, gestures, facial expressions, eye movement patterns, predicates or vocal tone, tempo or pitch.

'A' is the subject and leaves the room.

'B' decides to match one (or more) of the suggestions listed above and informs 'C'. 'B' recalls 'A', engaging 'A' in conversation, and paces and leads 'A'.

'C' observes and verifies that rapport has been established.

Rotate the roles.

Collateral Exercise #17

Purpose: To establish rapport with a student.

The teacher chooses a situation where he can have an opportunity to pace an individual student.

He decides to establish rapport by matching one or more of the following: body position, gestures, facial expressions, eye movement patterns, predicates or vocal tone, tempo or pitch.

The teacher engages the student in conversation and paces and leads the student. Verification of rapport occurs if the student follows the teacher's lead.

Exercise #18
Establishing Rapport

Purpose: To establish rapport through switching.

'A' is the subject and leaves the room.

'B' decides what to match through switching and informs 'C'. 'B' recalls 'A', engages 'A' in conversation and paces and leads 'A'.

'C' observes and verifies the establishment of rapport.

Rotate the roles.

Exercise #19
Establishing Rapport

Purpose: To establish rapport by matching vocal tone, tempo, timbre quality, intonation, word emphasis and words.

'A' states a sentence.

'B' repeats the sentence matching tone, tempo, timbre, quality, intonation, stress and words until 'C' indicates that matching has occurred.

'C' observes and acts as referee.

'A' states a total of three sentences, which 'B' matches.

Rotate the roles.

Collateral Exercise #18

Purpose: To establish rapport with a student by switching.

The teacher chooses a situation where he can have the opportunity to pace an individual student.

The teacher decides how he wants to establish rapport, engages the student in conversation and establishes rapport through a switching technique. He verifies the success of the switching technique by leading.

Collateral Exercise #19

Purpose: To subtly establish rapport by matching a student's vocal tone, tempo, timbre quality, and intonation.

The teacher chooses a situation where he can have the opportunity to track an individual student.

He engages the student in conversation and subtly paces the student by mirroring his vocal tone, tempo, timbre quality and intonation. The teacher then leads to verify the establishment of rapport.

Summary

Pacing can include the matching of voice tone, volume or tempo, the mirroring of eye movements, facial expressions, gestures, breathing, and body posture, and switching (where one sensory system is used to match another). Leading is used as a check to determine if rapport has been established. Leading occurs when a teacher subtly alters whatever he has been pacing. If students follow the teacher's lead, then rapport has been established.

Establishing rapport through pacing provides tools for teachers to:

Reduce student resistance

Achieve better classroom control

Prepare students for the installation of new learning patterns

Lead students into new learning situations.

Pacing helps to move students into a physiological state where learning can more readily occur.

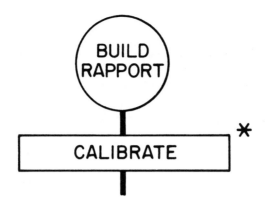

Chapter 10

CALIBRATION

Life presents numerous occasions that give us the opportunity to interpret data and to check the accuracy of our interpretations. Anyone working with tools quickly discovers that standard sockets applied to metric nuts will not work. Hunters know that ammunition only fits guns that are calibrated for that ammunition. Speedometers that do not register automobile speed accurately can result in inadvertent speeding and can lead to the receipt of traffic tickets. Reading the wrong side of a thermometer that has both Celsius and Fahrenheit readings can cause momentary confusion. Misreading data or being unable to draw conclusions from the available sensory data are even more obvious in human relations contexts. Students having difficulty learning to spell may lack a visual component in their spelling pattern. The teacher trained in calibrating involuntary eye movement patterns can quickly determine if students lack such a component and can then help students make adjustments that can result in spelling improvement. Determining the "real" message that people communicate with their sensory feedback separates the amateurs from the professionals!

What is "Calibration," and why is it necessary?

The term "calibration" refers to the ability to read non-verbal feedback and to associate it with an individual's internal state. It is an essential part of being a good communicator. This chapter emphasizes reading involuntary eye movements to determine which of the internal sensory systems students are utilizing at a particular moment. (For a review of eye movement patterns, consult Fig. 5 on page 52.) Once rapport has been established, the next step is to determine students' eye movement patterns. One way these patterns can be determined is to ask students certain questions and watch their involuntary eye movement response. Here are some examples of questions that could be asked to determine students' visual entry cues. The questions need not be answered verbally.

1)

V^r
{
What was the name of the last movie you attended?
... or book that you read?

What color are the eyes of your favorite person?

What is your favorite food?

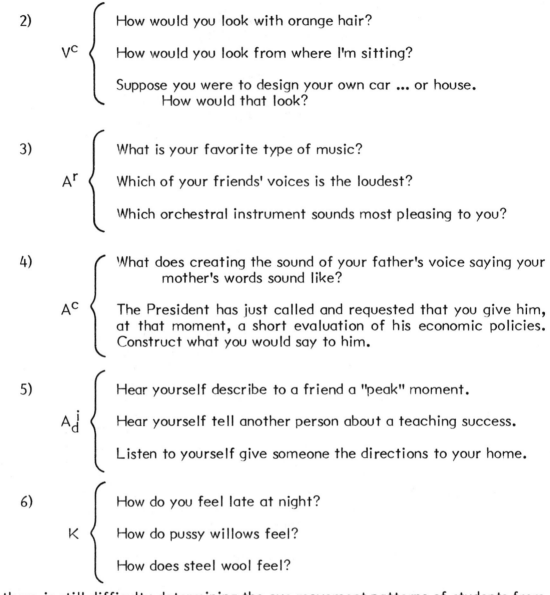

2) V^c
- How would you look with orange hair?
- How would you look from where I'm sitting?
- Suppose you were to design your own car ... or house. How would that look?

3) A^r
- What is your favorite type of music?
- Which of your friends' voices is the loudest?
- Which orchestral instrument sounds most pleasing to you?

4) A^c
- What does creating the sound of your father's voice saying your mother's words sound like?
- The President has just called and requested that you give him, at that moment, a short evaluation of his economic policies. Construct what you would say to him.

5) A_d^i
- Hear yourself describe to a friend a "peak" moment.
- Hear yourself tell another person about a teaching success.
- Listen to yourself give someone the directions to your home.

6) K
- How do you feel late at night?
- How do pussy willows feel?
- How does steel wool feel?

If there is still difficulty determining the eye movement patterns of students from these questions, try one of these methods. One method is to ask a more complex question. For example, if students come up with a movie title without the eyes shifting either upper left or upper right, then a more complex question could bring forth the information: "Was _____ the first or second movie that you've seen in the last two months?"

Another way to determine eye movement patterns is to ask students to move their eyes either up right or up left and ask in which eye position it is easier for them to remember the movie. "Is it easier to remember a movie scene up here (pointing), or up here?" This questioning can be done with each eye movement pattern. In most instances (perhaps 90% or 95% of most cases), all that really needs to be done is to identify the eye movement patterns for one direction. The patterns for the other direction will have to be the opposite of the ones that have already been determined. If the patterns vary, full calibration will need to be carried out to determine the individual's eye movement pattern.

Even though eye movement patterns can differ for right-handed people when compared with the diagram showing eye movement patterns for normally organized right-handed people, remember that each student's eye movement pattern will be consistent for that student. Knowing students' involuntary eye movement patterns will provide information about how they process and how they learn information.

Calibrating Elementary Students

Perhaps the easiest way to calibrate elementary students (and probably most students as well), is just to engage them in conversation. Calibration questions can usually be worked into the conversation without the teacher becoming transparent regarding his objective. If necessary, the more formal questions and techniques suggested earlier can be employed.

Exercise #20
Learning to Calibrate

Purpose: To increase sensory discrimination.

Phase I

'A' selects a person he likes and indicates when he is thinking about the person. ('A' does not name or describe the person.)

'B' watches for small changes in 'A's breathing, posture, facial expression, eye movement patterns, skin color, etc. and calibrates to 'A's sensory feedback.

'A' selects a person he dislikes and again indicates when he is thinking about the person. ('A' does not name or describe the person.)

'B' calibrates to 'A's sensory feedback.

'A' recalls each person as many times as it takes 'B' to calibrate.

'C' observes.

Phase II

'B' asks 'A' a series of comparative questions. For example:

"Which one is taller?"

"Which one is lighter?"

Which one has darker hair?"
(Continued)

Collateral Exercise #20

Purpose: To transfer sensory discrimination to the classroom.

The teacher selects several students and observes them throughout the day or over a period of a week.

Each time students access strong, but different states, the teacher compares their sensory feedback.

How, specifically, did their feedback differ in each state?

Exercise #20
Learning to Calibrate
(Continued)

'A' does not answer verbally, but thinks about which person best answers the questions.

'B' and 'C' watch 'A's sensory response and for each question write down the person they think 'A' has selected.

('A' may initially recall each person as he compares them to see which person best fits the answer to the question. He may nod his head to indicate when he has selected his answer.)

'B' and 'C' compare their answers with 'A's answer.

(To make this exercise more challenging, select people whom you mildly like and mildly dislike. The sensory changes will be more subtle.)

Rotate the roles.

Exercise #21
Learning to Calibrate

Purpose: To learn to calibrate to a person's sensory feedback.

'A' is the subject.

'B' faces 'A' and holds 'A's hands.

'C' observes.

'A' visualizes three different experiences. Each time he experiences a new experience, he squeezes 'B's hands. 'B' observes and calibrates 'A's sensory reactions.

'A' again goes through the experiences in the same order.

'A' visualizes all of the experiences again, but places them in a different order.

(Continued)

Collateral Exercise #21

Purpose: To transfer calibration skills to the classroom.

The teacher selects several students and observes them throughout the day or over the period of a week.

Each time these students access a strong, but different state, the teacher makes a mental snapshot of the state change and writes down sensory changes.

The teacher, at a later time, reviews the notes and visualizes in detail the students in their states. The teacher mixes the order of the states and visually recreates the students in their states.

The teacher physically duplicates the students in their states, right down to the smallest sensory feedback that he can recall.

Exercise #21
Learning to Calibrate
(Continued)

'B' guesses the correct order of the experiences. ('C' can indicate whether he agrees with 'B'.) 'A' indicates the order of the experiences.

'A' again visualizes the experiences in their original order.

'B' guesses the content of each experience (what he thinks 'A' was doing). 'A' reveals the nature of the experience.

Rotate the roles.

Exercise #22
Calibrating Eye Movement Patterns

Purpose: To learn to calibrate eye movement patterns.

'B' engages 'A' in conversation and identifies 'A's eye movement patterns,

or

'B' asks 'A' the following questions and identifies 'A's eye movement patterns.

V^r
- What was the name of the last movie you attended?
- What is your favorite beverage?

V^c
- How would you look dressed as Superman (or Wonder Woman)?
- Suppose you were to design your own classroom. How would that look?

(Continued)

Collateral Exercise #22

Purpose: To learn to calibrate students' eye movement patterns.

The teacher engages in conversation with several students, one at a time, and determines their eye movement patterns.

A^r {
What is your favorite type of music?

Which orchestral instrument sounds most pleasing to you?

A^c {
What does creating the sound of your father's voice saying your mother's words sound like?

A parent has just asked you to evaluate her son's academic performance in your class. Construct what you would say.

A$_d^i$ {
Hear yourself tell a parent what a pleasure it is having their son or daughter in your class.

Listen to yourself give someone the directions to your school.

K {
How does dried oatmeal feel?

How does a puppy feel?

Summary

The involuntary eye movements of a normally organized right-handed person facing the observer would be as follows:

Fig. 13: Summary of Eye Movement Patterns

V^r - upper right

V^c - upper left

A^r - mid right

A^c - mid left

A$_d^i$ - down right

K - down left

Calibration, attuning oneself to this involuntary eye movement pattern, can be accomplished by asking specific questions and by observing students' eye movement patterns. Knowing these eye movement patterns provides helpful information in using many of the techniques mentioned in this book. It is particularly vital in eliciting and installing learning patterns.

Notes

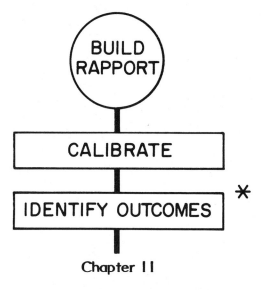

Chapter II

IDENTIFYING OUTCOMES

The Master addressed a group of student teachers. "Clearly determined outcomes," he stated, "are imperative not only in educational achievements, but in life as well. Because of my ability in assisting people in making changes, I have had many teachers and students seek my counsel," he continued. "During these sessions I frequently find that, even in their own minds, what they desire is poorly formulated. When people's outcomes are poorly formulated, my major objective is to ask them questions that are designed to help them clarify their outcomes. What frequently happens is that once they clarify their outcomes, they have an easier time achieving them. I remember a student teacher who was trying to make a decision about whether or not to become engaged to a particular young man. She was quite confused about whether he was the 'right' person for her, and whether she was too young and immature to take such a big step. As we sifted through all of her feelings to determine what it was that she desired, it became apparent to her that she lacked a clear-cut picture of what she wanted in a marriage. Consequently, she was confused about her own choice of a man. What was particularly interesting to me, was the change in her that occurred simply as a result of her clarifying her outcome. She was then able to make a decision that was truly beneficial to her."

"So it is," the Master concluded, "that by developing clearly determined outcomes, problem situations that appear complex and confusing in life are often revealed as simple situations for which solutions can easily be generated to solve them."

How does the teacher assist students in formulating outcomes?

Once rapport has been established and calibration has occurred, the next step is to collect information about the students' present state and their desired state. Entry cues can determine this information. Generally the Identifying Outcome Technique is used with individual students and is part of a pattern that may lead to the use of intervention techniques. (A group or a class could also use the identifying outcome procedure to aid them in developing the outcomes they seek.)

The three qualities of students' outcomes are: to make the outcome positive in content and in tone, achievable, and environmentally sound. Outcomes should be stated in a positive manner. Outcomes should also be achievable; they should be within the individuals' power to reach. Lastly, outcomes should fit within the environment in which the students function.

Next, the teacher proceeds to collect information. Four of the best ways to collect information include:

Asking questions that determine the outcome or desired state

Obtaining evidence that the student is accessing that state

Seeking information that clarifies the context in which the outcome is anticipated

Obtaining information that indicates with certainty whether the desired state is environmentally sound.

The questions follow:

1) Outcome Question:

"What do you want?" Sometimes students will answer in the negative. (Example: "I don't want to be so up-tight before the football game.") The teacher can guide the student toward a positive outcome by saying, "That's what you don't want. What is it that you want?", or by responding with feedback that would change the context of the statement to a positive one. (Example: "I want to be relaxed before the football game.")

2) Evidence Question:

"How would you know if you got it (the outcome)?" The information sought here is sensory information. For example, if the student sought to be relaxed when competing in an athletic event, sensory information indicating that he had achieved the outcome might be that he had a relaxed feeling in his stomach, that he was able to concentrate better, that there was an absence of internal dialogue, that he was not acting out his nervousness, or that his fellow athletes remarked about his calmness.

Additional methods for gathering specific evidence would include asking the following questions:

a) "When you have reached your outcome, what will you be doing?"

This question encourages the student to focus on his external behavior (K^e).

b) "When you have reached your outcome, what kinds of feelings will you be experiencing?"

This question helps the student focus on his internal feelings (K^i).

c) "When you have reached your outcome, what kinds of thoughts will you be thinking?"

This question focuses the student's concentration on his internal dialogue (A_d^i).

If these questions do not bring forth the necessary evidence, then switch to a more explicit behavioral frame by making this statement:

"Show me what you'd look like if you achieved _____." The student can then demonstrate behaviorally what the state would look like. It may be helpful for the teacher to make a mental snapshot (or image) of that state for future reference.

3) Context Questions:

"With whom do you want to experience this outcome?"

"Where do you want to experience this outcome?"

"When do you want to experience this outcome?"

While these questions may appear to be self-evident, asking them eliminates the possibility of incorrect assumptions ("mind reading") on the teacher's part.

4) Environmental Questions:

"What are the advantages in changing?"

"What are the disadvantages in changing?"
(Disadvantages are always involved in changing.)

These questions help ensure that the outcome will properly "fit" within the environmental system of the student. (Simplified outcome questions can be found on pg.227.)

Helping Elementary Students Identify Outcomes

Some elementary students may be able to answer the outcome questions without any modification of them. For those who have difficulty with the questions, teachers can modify them to make them more understandable. Another alternative would be to teach a class unit on goals - their desirability, how to develop them, etc.

In explaining goals to individual students, the teacher could elicit and discuss past goals which these students have achieved. The discussion of such goals should be made as concrete and as realistic as possible for the students. A discussion of the students' goals could and probably should include an emphasis upon the relationship of the sensory systems to the goal. Students can be asked what they saw, heard, felt and, if applicable, smelled and tasted. The students can then be led to discuss their present outcome(s) in as specific terms as possible. Attention can now be directed to what the students see, hear and feel (and if pertinent what they smell and taste). Using the dominant sensory system of the children by having them, if visual, draw a picture and/or write about the outcome; if auditory, having them talk about their goal to a friend; if kinesthetic, having them act out their goal.

Evidence questions could be dealt with in a similar fashion. By discussing a past goal that had been achieved, the teacher could discuss sensory information that the students conveyed that indicated to them that they had achieved their past goals. A transfer of the knowledge and awareness of achieving the past goals could be made to the current goal. The teacher could compare the two goals, pointing out the sensory goal and then he could assist them in obtaining the sensory evidence information from them for their present goal.

The environmental question could be introduced by discussing with the students that there were advantages and disadvantages connected with achieving their past goal. Once these advantages and disadvantages are drawn out, a comparison can be applied to the students' present goal and any advantages or disadvantages regarding the students present goal will be more readily evident to them.

Exercise #23
Outcome Drill

Purpose: To learn to change students' outcomes.

'A' chooses a particular state (agreement, happiness, etc.) and tells 'B' the state.

'B' demonstrates his concept of that state to 'C' while 'A' turns away.

'A' tries to put 'B' in that state with any means in 3 minutes.

'C' stands behind 'B' and uses a hand barometer to guide 'A'.

(Explanation:
A hand barometer means that 'C' is holding one arm straight out from his shoulder and is bending the arm at a 90° angle at the elbow, the hand pointing skyward. 'C's other hand is positioned palm downward and moves up and down from the elbow to the wrist. This arrangement acts as a gauge to let 'A' know when 'B' is behaviorally moving toward the state. The hand moves higher as 'A' successfully moves 'B' toward the state.)

Collateral Exercise #23

Purpose: To transfer outcome awareness to students.

The teacher selects one or more students. He determines an outcome state and throughout the course of the day, or over a period of several days, puts the student or students into that state at least once during the period or day. He may use any means at his disposal to achieve his outcome(s).

For additional challenges the teacher can put a group of students or a class into particular outcome states.

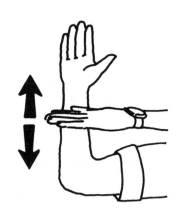

Exercise #24
"As If" Outcome Exercise

Purpose: To learn to change student's outcomes and to increase one's flexibility.

'A' chooses an outcome, and tells 'B' and 'C' the state associated with the outcome. (An outcome is a desirable goal that is consciously sought.)

'B' demonstrates the state.

'A' changes the outcome using as many ways as possible in 5 minutes. (This may include direct manipulation, statements like: "Have you ever ...?", or "Who do you know that represents X ?")

'C' stands behind 'B' and uses a hand barometer to indicate the success of the change effort.

Exercise #25
"As If" Outcome Exercise

Purpose: To learn to use the "As If" outcome.

Phase I

'A' selects six personal problems and writes them on one side of a folded sheet of paper. 'A' then chooses one problem.

'B' asks 'A' these questions:

> "Why do you have it?"
> "Who causes it?"
> "Who's to blame?"
> "What are the obstacles or limitations to solving the problem?"

'C' observes.

(Continued)

Collateral Exercise #24

Purpose: To transfer learning to change a student's outcome in a classroom setting.

The teacher selects a student and has that student formulate an outcome about something. The student demonstrates the state.

The teacher changes the outcome-state using as many ways as possible, in a 5 minute period.

Collateral Exercise #25

Purpose: To learn to use the "As If" technique in the classroom.

The teacher selects a student who is interested in changing some aspect of his behavior. Once the outcome has been determined, the teacher can say:

> "Let's pretend that it's three months from now.
> "What outcome(s) have you achieved?"
> "Which resources have you acquired that allow you to reach your outcome(s)?"
> "What are the possibilities now?"
> "What was the first step you took in achieving your outcome?"

If, as a result of the questions, the outcome has changed, help the student clarify it.

Phase II

'A' uses the same problem.

'B' asks the following set of questions and notes 'A's sensory changes between his present state and the outcome state. 'B' acts "as if" the problem is solved:

> "What outcome(s) have you already achieved?"
> "Which resources have you acquired that enable you to reach the outcome?"
> "What specifically demonstrated to you that you achieved your outcome?" ("What let you know at the moment that you were successful?")
> "What are the possibilities now?"
> "What was the first step in achieving your outcome?"

Phase III

On the other side of the folded paper, 'A' writes down the potential outcome of each of the six problems, opposite the six questions previously listed. 'A' then states each outcome verbally.

'B' looks for sensory evidence to support each outcome.

If the outcomes have been modified, 'C' writes down the modification. 'C' summarizes each situation and then asks 'A' for the advantages and disadvantages of each solution.

Exercise #26 - Eliciting a Well-Formed Outcome by Future Pacing

Purpose: To learn to develop a well-formed outcome through future pacing.

'A' makes an outcome statement.

'B' accepts the statement and future paces by asking these questions:

"Is this what you wanted?"
"Now that you have achieved ___,

what disadvantages have you experienced?"
how are you different?"
how are things going now?"
is not having this benefiting you in some way?"

(In this process, 'A' may change his outcome); 'C' writes down 'A's first outcome and final outcome statements. 'C' also challenges any irrelevant statements and checks to be certain that 'B' and 'A' stay in the future tense.

Exercise #27
Eliciting a Well-Formed Outcome

Purpose: To elicit a well-formed outcome.

'B' elicits a positive outcome statement from 'A' by asking:

"What do you want?"

If necessary, 'B' helps 'A' to make a positive statement.

'B' elicits sensory information by asking 'A' this question:

"How would you know when you get it?"

(Continued)

Collateral Exercise #26

Purpose: To elicit from a student a well-formed outcome by future pacing.

The teacher selects a student who would like to change some aspect of his behavior. The teacher has the student make an outcome statement and writes down the outcome. He accepts the outcome statement and future paces by asking the student these questions:

"Now that you have achieved ____,

what disadvantages have you experienced?"
how are you different?"
how are things going now?"
is not having this benefiting you in some way?"

This process may result in a changed outcome. Any change in the outcome can be determined by comparing the final outcome with the original one.

Collateral Exercise #27

Purpose: To elicit a well-formed outcome from a student.

The teacher selects a student who seeks a behavioral change.

He elicits a positive outcome statement by asking the following questions:

"What do you want?"
"How would you know when you get it (the outcome)?"

If necessary, the teacher can ask these three questions to gather more specific evidence:

"When you have reached your outcome, what will you be doing?"

(Continued)

Exercise #27
Eliciting a Well-Formed Outcome
(Continued)

If necessary, 'B' can ask these three questions to 'A':

"When you have reached your outcome, what will you be doing?"

"When you have reached your outcome, what kinds of feelings will you be experiencing?"

"When you have reached your outcome, what kinds of thoughts will you be thinking?"

If needed, 'B' has 'A' demonstrate the state, and 'B' elicits the necessary sensory evidence by observing 'A'.

'B' asks 'A' the Context Questions:

"With whom do you want to experience this outcome?"
"Where do you want to experience this outcome?"
"When do you want to experience this outcome?"

'B' asks 'A' the Environmental Questions:

"What are the advantages in changing?"
"What are the disadvantages in changing?"

Collateral Exercise #27
(Continued)

"When you have reached your outcome, what kinds of feelings will you be experiencing?"
"When you have reached your outcome, what kind of thoughts will you be thinking?"

If necessary, the teacher can have the student demonstrate the state and elicit the necessary sensory evidence by asking the student to:

"Show me what you'd look like if you achieved _____."

The teacher next asks the Context Questions:

"With whom do you want to experience this outcome?"
"Where do you want to experience this outcome?"
"When do you want to experience this outcome?"

The final questions are the Environmental Questions:

"What are the advantages in changing?"
"What are the disadvantages in changing?"

Summary

Helping students identify positive outcomes contributes to creating states in which they may more effectively seek their outcomes. Students will, for example, be more aware of what resources are needed to achieve their outcomes, they will also be able to make wise decisions about preferred ways to realize their outcomes. Assisting students in identifying positive outcomes is accomplished by asking the students a number of questions that serve as guidelines. On some occasions, the questions may be powerful enough to bring about the desired changes without resorting to more sophisticated techniques.

Notes

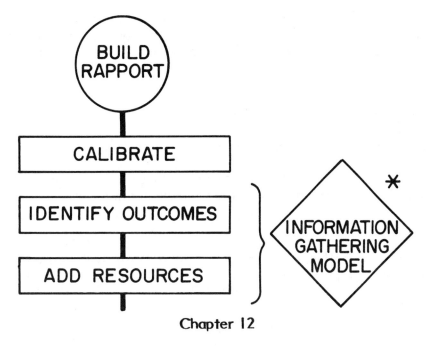

Chapter 12

THE INFORMATION GATHERING MODEL

The teacher had asked to see the junior high student to discuss some problems that she had with her homework. In the conversation that followed, the teacher realized that the personal problems of the young girl were affecting her school work. "She doesn't like me any more! She's not a real friend! She doesn't make me feel good! Every time I'm with her lately she treats me like a baby. I should find another friend!" These were typical comments made by the student. Because the student spoke in such generalized terms the teacher quietly and symphathetically sought more specific information. In this way he helped to connect the student's language and her sensory experience, and as this process occurred, the student developed a more complete understanding of what she could do to improve relations with her friend. Shortly thereafter she reported to the teacher that the relationship with the friend was "...better than ever!" The fact that she was getting her homework completed in time confirmed her statement.

What is the "Information Gathering Model?" What is its purpose? How is it used?"

Each of us creates his own perception or model of the world. To create these models, our internal experience must interact constantly with our external, or sensory experience. Language serves as a connection between our external and our sensory experience. The Information Gathering Model (IG Model) uses linguistic information gathering techniques to help students reconnect their sensory experiences with their language.

Fig. 14: <u>IG Model</u>

LANGUAGE BRIDGES THE GAP SENSORY EXPERIENCE

This gap between students' language and their sensory experience can be bridged. Ask challenging questions of students who use unspecified nouns, unspecified verbs, universal quantifiers, modal operators of possibility and necessity, and nominalizations. These challenging questions are interspersed throughout this chapter. The IG Model can be used in three ways:

1) by itself as a separate set of tools;
2) as part of the Identification Outcome Frame; or
3) as part of the Adding Resources Frame.

The sensory exercises at the end of this chapter provide efficient and rapid ways to integrate automatic responses to each of the following categories.

1. Unspecified Nouns

The use of unspecified nouns means that students have introduced unspecified persons, places, or things in sentences. The IG Model challenging questions for unspecified nouns are: "Who specifically?" or "What specifically?" or "Which specifically?".

Example	Challenge
"People are very interesting."	"Who, specifically, is interesting?"
"They are very kind to me."	"Who, specifically, is kind to you?"
"That city is the greatest!"	"Which city, specifically, is the greatest?"
"That place is terrific!"	"Which place, specifically, is terrific?"
"That thing is in the way."	"What thing, specifically, is in the way?"
"That class is very stimulating."	"What class, specifically, is stimulating?"

The challenging questions force students to identify unspecified persons, places, or things, thus providing a more comprehensive representation of the students' experience.

2. Unspecified Verbs

Like unspecified nouns, the term unspecified verbs means that verbs are introduced in a sentence but are not clarified. The IG Model challenging question for unspecified verbs is: "How specifically?"

Example	Challenge
"We really clobbered them!"	"How, specifically, did you clobber them?"
"They encourage me to score points."	"How, specifically, do they encourage you?"

"He supported me."   "How, specifically?"

The challenge forces students to be exact, again providing a more comprehensive representation of their experiences.

3. Universal Quantifiers

Universal quantifiers include the use of such words as:

all	none
every	never
each	no one
always	nothing
any	nobody

When students use universal quantifiers, they tend to increase the magnitude of their generalizations to the point where they may limit themselves. The IG Model challenge can consist of two or three responses: a vocal exaggeration of the universal quantifier, e.g., "All?"; and two questions: "Has there ever been an example of when it doesn't _____?", or "Has there ever been an example of when it does _____?"

Example	Challenge
"All of us are going."	"All of you? or "Do you know of anyone who isn't going?"
"Anyone can see that!"	"Absolutely anyone can see that?" or "Can you think of a time when someone couldn't see that?"
"Each of us should make a lot of money."	"Each of us?" or "Can you think of a similar circumstance when that didn't happen?"
"None of you should do it!"	"None of us?" or "Do you know anyone who does it?"

By challenging the students' universal quantifiers, the teacher helps students become aware of having more options to consider.

4. Modal Operators of Possibility and Necessity

Modal operators of possibility denote feelings of inability to do what is desired. Modal operators of necessity imply that in their assessment of the situation students have no other options open to them. Modal operators of possibility and necessity include the following:

Possibility	Necessity
can't	have to
impossible	necessary
unable	must
couldn't	should
no way	no choice
	forced to

Use of modal operators limit individuals' choices. The IG Model challenge for modal operators of possibility is "What stops you from ...?" The challenges for the modal operators of necessity are: What would happen if you did ...?" and "What would happen if you didn't ...?"

Example	Challenge
"It's impossible to complete that assignment by the due date."	"What's preventing you from completing it?"
"I'm unable to explain the directions thoroughly."	"What's stopping you from explaining them?"
"I have to get an 'A' on the next test."	"What would happen if you didn't?"
"I should write that paper now."	"What would happen if you did?"

As with the universal quantifiers, challenging the modal operators makes students aware of having more alternatives.

5. Nominalizations

Nominalizations are verbs that have been transformed into nouns. The IG Model challenge for nominalizations is to change the noun back into a verb.

Example	Challenge
"I need loving."	"How would you like to be loved?"
"That's excitement!"	"In what way are you excited?"
"I don't get any respect."	"How would you like to be respected?"
"Efficiency is most significant."	"Who's being efficient and in what way?"

The effect of the challenge is to make students aware that what they thought of as a finished event is, in reality, a continuing process.

6. Cause and Effect

Cause and effect statements indicate that students uttering the statement believe that an action on the part of another person has directly affected their emotion and that they have a limited response within a particular situation. The IG Model challenge to cause and effect statements is to ask:

Example	Challenge
"When you smile at me, it makes my day."	"How does my smiling at you make your day?"
"When you look at me, I want to work harder."	"How does my looking at you make you want to work harder?"
"Your talking annoys me."	"How does my talking annoy you?"
"You challenge me."	"How do I challenge you?"

Challenging the cause and effect statements allows students to consider other response options.

Exercise #28 - Integrating Plural Nouns & Past Tense Verbs

Purpose: To integrate plural nouns and past tense verbs.

Phase I

'A', 'B' and 'C' each develop a list of plural nouns and past tense verbs and each construct separate sentences for the plural nouns and past tense verbs.

'B' reads his list of plural nouns.

'A' lifts the index finger of his right hand each time a plural noun is read.

'C' watches to see that 'A' responds correctly.

Phase II

'B' reads his list of past tense verbs.

'A' lifts the second finger of his right hand each time a past tense verb is read.

'C' observes.

Phase III

'B' scrambles the plural noun and past tense verb lists.
(Continued)

Collateral Exercises #28 and #29

Purpose: To learn to identify students' use of plural nouns and past tense verbs.

The teacher identifies plural nouns and past tense verbs as often as he can when students state them.

If necessary to the integration process, each time he hears a plural noun, the teacher lifts the index fingers of his right hand. Each time he hears a past tense verb, he lifts the second finger of his right hand.

Exercise #28 - Integrating
Plural Nouns & Past Tense Verbs
(Continued)

'A' identifies the plural nouns with the index finger and the past tense verbs with the second finger when they are read.

'C' observes and, if necessary, corrects 'A'.

Rotate the roles.

Exercise #29 - Continuing the
Integration of Plural Nouns
and Past Tense Verbs

Purpose: To continue the integration of plural nouns and past tense verbs.

Phase I

'B' reads his plural noun sentences.

'A' lifts the index finger of his right hand each time a plural noun is read.

'C' observes.

Phase II

'B' reads his past tense verb sentences.

'A' lifts the second finger of his right hand each time a past tense verb is read.

'C' functions the same as in Phase I.

Phase III

'B' scrambles the plural nouns and past tense verb sentences.

'A' identifies the plural nouns with the index finger and the past tense verbs with the second finger each time they are used.

'C' observes and, if necessary, corrects 'A'.

Rotate the roles.

Exercise #30 – Integrating Universal Quantifiers and Modal Operators

Purpose: To integrate universal quantifiers and modal operators.

Phase I

'B' reads the following list of universal quantifiers twice:

all	none
every	never
each	no one
any	nothing
always	nobody

'A' raises the third finger on his right hand each time a universal quantifier is read.

'C' observes.

Phase II

'B' reads the following list of modal operators of possibility and necessity twice:

Possibility	Necessity
can't	have to
impossible	necessary
unable	must
couldn't	should
no way	no choice
	forced to

'A' raises the fourth finger on his right hand each time a modal operator is read.

'C' observes.

Phase III

'B' makes sentences using the universal quantifiers and the modal operators. 'B' then scrambles the sentences.

'A' identifies the quantifiers and the operators by raising the appropriate finger when they are mentioned.

(Continued)

Collateral Exercise #30

Purpose: To learn to identify student use of universal quantifiers and modal operators.

The teacher identifies universal quantifiers and modal operators as often as he can when students state them.

If necessary to further the integration process, the teacher slightly raises his third finger each time he hears a universal quantifier, and his fourth finger each time he hears a modal operator.

Exercise #30 - Integrating Universal Quantifiers and Modal Operators
(Continued)

'C' observes and, if necessary, corrects 'A'.

Rotate the roles.

Exercise #31 - Installing Challenges For Plural Nouns and Past Tense Verbs

Purpose: To install challenges for plural nouns and past tense verbs.

Phase I

'A', 'B' and 'C' individually install the following challenges for plural nouns on the index finger of their left hand. Each time after they read to themselves a plural noun, they ask the following appropriate question and at the same time slightly raise the index finger of the left hand.

> "Who, specifically ...?"
> "What, specifically ...?"

Phase II

'A', 'B' and 'C' individually install the following challenge for past tense verbs on the second finger of the left hand. Each time after they read to themselves a past tense verb, they ask the following question and at the same time slightly raise the second finger of the left hand.

> "How, specifically?"

Collateral Exercise #31

Purpose: To challenge students' use of plural nouns and past tense verbs.

Each time students use plural nouns and past tense verbs the teacher asks the appropriate challenges.

> "Who, specifically ...?"
>   or
> "What, specifically ...?"

Each time the teacher hears a past tense verb being used, he asks the challenge:

> "How, specifically ...?"

Exercise #32 - Installing Challenges For Universal Quantifiers and Modal Operators

Purpose: To install challenges for universal quantifiers and modal operators.

Phase I

'A', 'B' and 'C' individually install the following challenges for universal quantifiers on the third finger of the left hand. Each time after they read to themselves a universal quantifier, they ask one of the following questions and at the same time slightly raise the third finger of the left hand.

> "All ...?"
>
>   exaggeration
>
> "Every ...?"
>
> "Is there ever an example of when it doesn't _____?" "Or does _____?"

Phase II

'A', 'B' and 'C' individually install the following challenges for modal operators on the fourth finger of the left hand. Each time after they read to themselves a modal operator, they ask the appropriate question and at the same time slightly raise the fourth finger of the left hand.

> #### Possibility
>
> "What stops you?"
>
> #### Necessity
>
> "What would happen if you did?"
> "What would happen if you didn't?"

Collateral Exercise #32

Purpose: To challenge students' use of universal quantifiers and modal operators.

Each time students use universal quantifiers, the teacher uses the apropriate challenge.

> "All ...?"
>
> "Every ...?"
>   or
> "Is there ever an example of when it doesn't _____?" "Or does _____?"

Each time students use modal operators, the teacher uses the appropriate challenge:

> "What stops you?"
> "What would happen if you did?"
> "What would happen if you didn't?"

Exercise #33
Integration Exercise

Purpose: To integrate the identification and challenges associated with the IG Model.

'B' scrambles and reads the sentences beginning with the plural nouns and ending with the modal operators.

'A' identifies plural nouns, past tense verbs, universal quantifiers and modal operators by raising the appropriate finger of the right hand. He then gives the appropriate challenge for each while raising the appropriate finger of the left hand.

'C' checks 'A' and, if necessary, corrects and assists 'A'.

Rotate the roles.

Exercise #34
Checking For Congruence

Purpose: To check for congruence between demonstrated states and other concepts of those states.

'A' selects a nominalization (happy, excited, etc.)

'B' physically demonstrates his concept of 'A's nominalization by modeling the nominalization.

'A' decides if 'B's concept of the nominalization matches his concept. If it doesn't, 'A' can physically demonstrate for 'B' and also verbally coach.

'C' observes.

Rotate the roles.

Collateral Exercise #33

Purpose: To challenge students' use of plural nouns, past tense verbs, universal quantifiers, and modal operators.

When students use plural nouns, past tense verbs, universal quantifiers, and modal operators, the teacher makes the appropriate challenge.

Collateral Exercises #34 and #35

Purpose: To challenge students using nominalizations and cause and effect statements.

When students use nominalizations the teacher makes the appropriate challenge.

When students use cause and effect statements the teacher challenges by asking:

"How does ___ cause ___?"

Exercise #35 – Contrasting
Past and Present Nominalizations

Purpose: To contrast the differences between past and present nominalizations.

'A' identifies nominalizations that are now part of his experiences. Then 'A' recalls a past experience and finds a time when he didn't have the nominalization.

'B' asks 'A': "What are the differences?"; "What enabled you to achieve the outcome?"

'C' observes.

Rotate the roles.

The Information Gathering Model and The Classroom

Use the IG Model in any context where more specific information is sought. These situations could include: individual conferences with students and/or parents, student-sharing situations (Share and Tell, "Bring and Brag," Magic Circle, Class Meetings), problem-solving experiences, incidents when the student needs assistance in determining outcomes, team sessions, or any occasions in which the outcome is to evaluate the students.

Summary

Assisting students in reconnecting their sensory experiences with their language is the purpose of the challenging questions utilized in the Information Gathering Model. When unspecified nouns, unspecified verbs, universal quantifiers, modal operators and nominalizations are used, both the students and the listener lack precise information for communication. The challenging questions allow for a more comprehensive representation of the students' experiences, give students more options to consider and make them aware that most of life's events are continuing processes rather than finished events. The IG Model can be used separately, or in conjunction with either Identifying Outcomes or with Adding Resources.

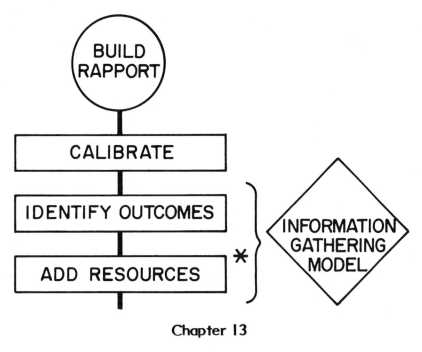

Chapter 13

ADDING RESOURCES

The Wizard of Oz is one of the great children's classics of all time. Most of us are familiar with the details of the story. After Dorothy and her friends accomplish the task assigned to them by the Wizard, they discover that he is a fraud. However, he is successful as a clever and wise psychologist. He points out to the Scarecrow, the Tin Woodsman, and the Cowardly Lion that the resources they seek have actually been with them all along. To the Scarecrow, the Wizard states that "anyone can have a brain, but what you lack is a diploma." So the Wizard awards him a Th.D., "Doctor of Thinkology." The Cowardly Lion is instructed not to "...confuse courage with wisdom." The Wizard says that the Lion is courageous enough but only lacks a medal, so he awards the Lion the "Triple Cross" which makes him part of the "Legion of Courage." The Tin Woodsman is given a heart (a clock), and the Wizard offers him these words of wisdom: "A heart is not judged, my sentimental friend, by how much you love, but by how much you are loved by others." By awarding the diploma, the medal, and the heart, the Wizard generated in Dorothy's friends the confidence they needed to maximize the qualities they already possessed. Often what our students think they lack is already a part of their experiences. Like the Wizard, we too can find ways to make our students aware of this "truth."

What are "Resources?" What is the reason for adding "Resources?" How is this accomplished?

Once the outcome is identified, the teacher asks students an additional question: "What personal resources do you need to achieve _____(your outcome)?" Each of us has relied on personal resources in the past to assist us in achieving our goals. These resources can be internal or external in nature. Internal resources depending upon the situation, could include:

persistence	tenderness	joy	decisiveness
stubbornness	helpfulness	confidence	love
strength	inflexibility	compassion	humor
flexibility	organization	disassociation	cleverness
happiness	adventurousness	anger	caring

External resources could include:

the acquisition of physical skills
strength
endurance
quickness
speed
models of people who exemplify the goal or,
various external stimuli which trigger a
particular response.

Usually, students will list several resources. If students have trouble selecting resources, the teacher can suggest several resources that might be appropriate. Students are free to accept or to disregard the suggested resources.

Another method of incorporating resources is to have students select resources and to act "as if" the outcome has already been achieved. The teacher uses the future tense in his conversation: "It's now three months from this date. You've achieved your outcome. What was the first step that you took to achieve it? What did you do after that? What was the third step?", etc. Asking students questions and acting "as if" the outcome has already been achieved may show students the outcome is achieveable. The "As If" approach could eliminate the need for any further intervention.

A third alternative is for the teacher to ask: "Is there someone you know who can exhibit __X__ (the outcome)?" Usually there will be someone. Ask students to picture this person doing __X__ in movie form and ask them to imagine themselves having the experience by pretending to step inside the person's body. If students are unable to think of anyone who has the particular resources that they would like to tap, ask them to select a particular person -- even an imaginary one -- and picture an imaginary situation in which the person is exhibiting the response. Instruct the students to imagine this person doing __X__ in movie form. Then, instruct the students to step into the person's body and achieve __X__.

A fourth alternative may be used when students have difficulty matching resources with experiences that they have had. The teacher gives these instructions: "I want you to carefully search your mind for an experience that you have had that either incorporates _____ (the entire resource), or an experience that partially incorporates _____." Once students acquire the resource base, the teacher can then decide what intervention would assist the students in achieving their outcome(s).

These same techniques can be used with elementary students. To be successful in adding resources, the elementary teacher will, of course, need to use language and explanations that relate to the students' models of the world.

Exercise #36
Generating Resources

Purpose: To learn to help others generate resources.

'A' states a desired and well-formed outcome.

'B' selects one or more of the alternative methods (as needed) of generating resources mentioned in this chapter and proceeds to assist 'A' in generating the needed resources.

'C' observes and, if necessary, coaches.

Rotate the roles.

Collateral Exercise #36

Purpose: To help students generate needed resources.

The teacher has a student desiring a behavioral change state a desired and well-formed outcome.

The teacher selects one or more of the alternative methods (as needed) of generating resources mentioned in this chapter and proceeds to assist students in generating the needed resources.

Summary

Adding internal and external resources to students' outcomes is an important step. On an unconscious basis, students' resources are being activated to achieve their outcomes. On a conscious basis, the students are beginning to realize that they may have the inner resources to achieve the outcomes that have eluded them.

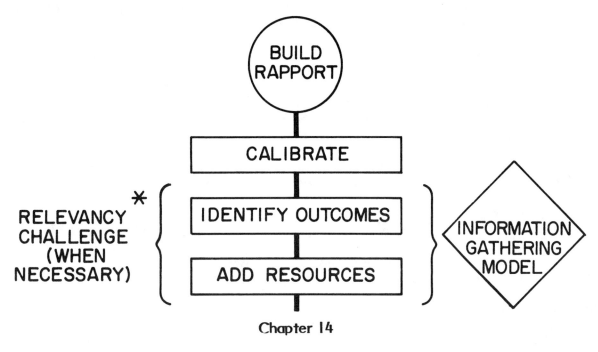

Chapter 14

THE RELEVANCY CHALLENGE

Two teachers were engaged in "shop talk" in the teachers' lounge. Mike began discussing his frustrations about the classroom behavior of a particular student that both he and Sheila taught. Sheila was surprised, because the student's behavior in her classroom was acceptable to her. As the conversation continued, Mike delved into the family history of the student, the student's home life, his personal appearance, and he made generalizations about "... that type student always being a troublemaker." Each time that Mike brought up what she considered information that had little bearing on the situation, and that tended to obscure it, Sheila gently but firmly challenged the relevancy of his statements. Mike finally admitted that he was somewhat reluctant to examine his relationship with the student because he felt he might be at fault. Clearing away the "smokescreen" caused Mike to examine, and ultimately, to improve his relationship with his student.

What is the "Relevancy Challenge?" How is it used?

The Relevancy Challenge is designed to be used any time it is needed from the Outcome Frame through the Resource Frame. The basic purpose of the Relevancy Challenge is to keep the conversation "on track" and prevent any digressions. The challenge is simply stated: "I appreciate your comment, but I'm uncertain about how your comment applies to what we are discussing.", or "I'm not sure what this information has to do with our discussion."

The use of the Relevancy Challenge can generate a number of results. One possible result is that the Relevancy Challenge, by not allowing students to hide behind irrelevant material, can force them to the real outcome more rapidly, and that action can precipitate rapid change. For example, students can be reluctant to establish an outcome because they may be afraid of how the changes will affect them. The student starts discussing what appears to be irrelevant information, perhaps telling a story or two. The teacher gently says, "Jim, your story is interesting but I'm not sure how it relates to what we're discussing." Either the student will make the connection, or he will stop telling the story. Without anything to use as concealment, students can move more quickly to deal with their feelings and to achieve their outcome(s).

The Relevancy Challenge can promote connections between feelings and events, and it can bring out any "hidden agenda" that may be present. If, in the previous example, the teacher used the Relevancy Challenge and the students were able to point out some feelings of fear that they had about achieving their outcome(s), the Relevancy Challenge could well demonstrate either the connection between feelings and events, or the "hidden agenda" or both.

The Relevancy Challenge is also an excellent tool to keep meetings running efficiently and can be used to keep classroom discussion on track.

Exercise #37 – Learning To Use The Relevancy Challenge

Purpose: to learn how to use the Relevancy Challenge with a student.

'A' states a desired outcome, but in the process adds irrelevant answers, stories, and/or material to the conversation.

'B', when necessary, uses appropriate Relevancy Challenges in a friendly manner.

'C' observes and, if necessary, coaches.

Rotate the roles.

Collateral Exercise #37

Purpose: To use the Relevancy Challenge with students.

The teacher has a conference with a student desiring a behavioral change. If necessary, the teacher uses the Relevancy Challenge in a positive and friendly manner.

Exercise #38 – Learning To Use The Relevancy Challenge

Purpose: To learn to use the Relevancy Challenge in a classroom discussion.

'A' and 'C' role play a typical classroom discussion and, at times, make irrelevant comments.

'B' uses appropriate Relevancy Challenges.

Rotate the roles.

Collateral Exercise #38

Purpose: To use the Relevancy Challenge in a Classroom discussion.

The teacher initiates a classroom discussion. If opportunities arise, he uses the Relevancy Challenge in a friendly and positive manner.

Summary

Irrelevant comments and digressions can derail the teacher's helpful efforts. Relevancy Challenges, when used in a positive and friendly manner, can keep individual conferences and classroom discussions on target.

Notes

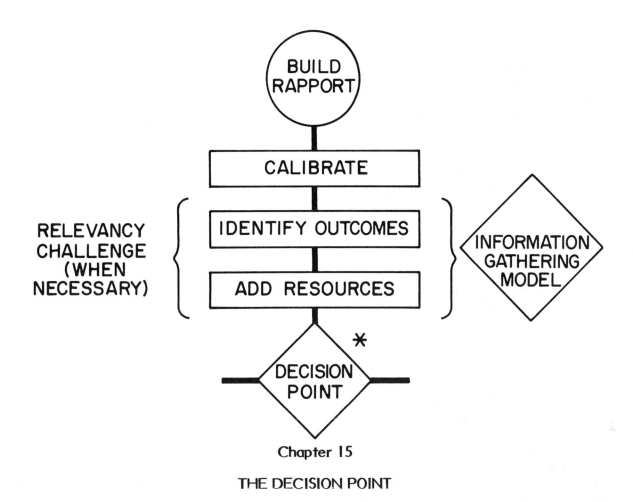

Chapter 15

THE DECISION POINT

The Master and his student had a close relationship. The student had frequently sought the Master's aid in helping him make personal changes. Because the changes had worked so well, the student trusted the Master. Now, the student approached the Master with a dilemma. Ordinarily, the student was conscientious and interested in his studies, but in one particular class he was not completing his homework. His grades were also beginning to slip and since he wanted to attend college, he needed to keep a high grade-point average. Some of his friends encouraged his irresponsibility and made him feel part of their group. The student wanted to develop a better attitude, but felt that he was unable to do so by himself.

Aware that his decision was critical, the Master carefully deliberated which technique would best accomplish what the student desired. Since part of the student sought change and part of him was gaining something from his irresponsible action, the Master selected a technique that would assist the student in generating new responses for that part of him that was responding negatively to the class. As he had anticipated, the technique worked and the Master felt a surge of satisfaction knowing that he had once again been of service to a student.

What is the "Decision Point?" When is the "Decision Point" reached? What options are then available to the teacher?

After the students have been led through the sequence of steps beginning with building rapport and ending with adding resources, the teacher needs to make a decision about which technique to use that will best meet the student's needs. At this juncture the teacher can view the Decision Point Frame in two contexts: Remedial and Developmental.

The **Remedial Frame,** as the name implies, indicates that a specific outcome is needed in a specific situation; or one change is needed in one context; or something broken needs to be fixed. Starting from the most basic to the more advanced, the five Remedial Frame techniques are as follows:

1) Linking
2) Combining Links
3) Integrating Links
4) Revising Life Patterns
5) Disassociation.

Examples of situations that fall within the Remedial Frame would be test anxiety in one subject, lack of motivation and poor attitude toward one subject, toward one school, toward one peer, toward one teacher.

The **Developmental Frame** implies that a specific outcome is sought in more than one context and that students, with the teacher's instruction, can learn to "develop" or create outcomes for themselves. The five Developmental Frame Techniques are:

1) Transforming
2) Eliciting Learning Patterns
3) Installing Learning Patterns
4) Metaphor Usage.
5) Submodality Patterns

Examples of situations falling into the Developmental Frame would include: poor motivation in general, poor attitude toward several people, most or all subjects and school in general, under-achievement in most subjects, unworkable or non-existent subject matter learning patterns, and any behavior incorporating secondary gain.

The procedure to follow is to:

1) identify whether the outcome is remedial or developmental;

2) start with the simplest technique to achieve the outcome within that particular frame, and use that technique.

> In the case of the Remedial Frame, the most simple technique would be linking, the most elaborate would be disassociation. In the Developmental Frame, transforming would be the most simple technique, whereas installing learning patterns or constructing and using a metaphor or using submodalities to change behavior would be the most elaborate. If, for any reason, the simplest technique should not work, then the next most advanced technique can be utilized. Situations that do not respond to the Integrating Links Technique may respond to the Transforming Technique.

The specific steps for each technique follow in the next two chapters.

REMEMBER, THE ONLY TIME THAT YOU CAN MAKE A MISTAKE IS IF YOU QUIT TRYING! At times, your intervention efforts may seem as though they are not succeeding. Therefore, either repeat the technique, particularly if you question how well it was done, or switch to another more advanced technique.

Exercise #39 – Learning To Decide Whether To Use Remedial or Developmental Techniques

Purpose: To learn to decide whether to use Remedial or Developmental techniques in achieving a desired outcome.

'A' states a desired outcome.

'B' determines whether a Remedial or Developmental technique would be most helpful in achieving the outcome. 'B' discusses the reason(s) for his choice with 'C'.

'C' discusses his reasons for agreeing or disagreeing with 'B'.

Collateral Exercise #39

Purpose: To decide whether to use Remedial or Developmental Techniques with students.

The teacher helps the student form a well-developed outcome. He then decides whether a Remedial or a Developmental Technique is most appropriate to use to achieve the outcome.

Summary

After laying the necessary groundwork which includes building rapport, calibrating, identifying outcomes and adding resources, the Decision Point represents an exciting time! The teacher has the opportunity to use either Remedial or Developmental Frame techniques. The function of the Remedial Frame is to change patterns of behavior where one change is needed in one context. The function of the Developmental Frame is to create new patterns of behavior that are desired in more than one context. At times, certain problems may overlap between the two frames. The problem of poor attitude, depending on its cause or longevity, could be easily solved by the Revising Life Patterns technique which falls within the Remedial Frame. If, however, there was strong secondary gain associated with the poor attitude, then Transforming, a Developmental Frame technique would be the logical choice to use as the change technique.

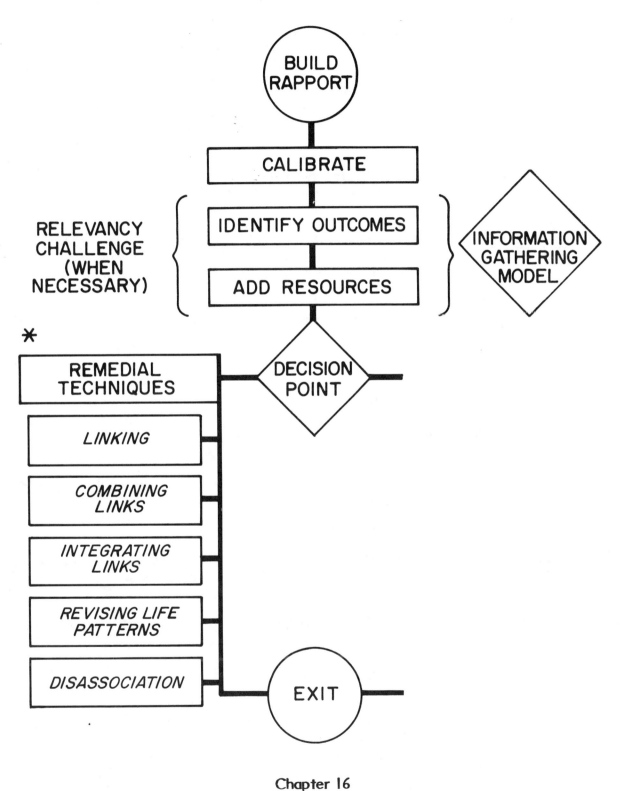

Chapter 16

REMEDIAL TECHNIQUES

It was demonstration time in one of my classes. At the beginning of the class students had written down several behaviors that they wished to change. Now one student had an opportunity to have that behavior changed. The volunteer wished to change her fear and uncomfortable feelings (not phobic feelings), that she experienced when she went into balconies and other high places. This was an ideal situation for the Integrating Links technique, so I went through the process with her. Twenty minutes later, her sensory feedback indicated an end to the problem. Not fully trusting what her sensory feedback told them, some members of the class proposed a test of the situation. During lunch time they had the subject walk out on a second-story fire escape. Ordinarily this would have caused traumatic feelings for her, but a behavioral change had occurred and she easily accomplished this task <u>without</u> her usual fearful/uncomfortable feelings!

What student responses indicate the need for "Remedial Techniques?"
What are "Remedial Techniques" and how are they utilized?

Remedial Techniques are used to deal with responses that call for a <u>single change in a single context</u>. Responses falling into the Remedial category could include <u>newly developed</u> test anxiety, lack of motivation, and a negative attitude toward school, or a teacher. The five **Remedial Techniques** are as follows:

1) **Linking**

2) **Combining Links**

3) **Integrating Links**

4) **Revising Life Patterns**

5) **Disassociation.**

Before these techniques are employed, it is assumed that all the steps from Building Rapport through The Decision Point, with the exception of Adding Resources, have been completed. Resources are added during the implementation of the majority of these techniques.

Linking

Linking occurs when a stimulus creates a highly predictable pattern of behavior from an individual. Links can be tied to any of the sensory systems and can be internal or external in their representation.

Recall some of the links that affect us. Some visual links inevitably cause us to make a particular response. Facial expressions of friends or loved ones, certain gestures of those we know and visual symbols like our flag serve as visual links to many of us. Auditory links affecting us could include particular songs, our national anthem, parental voices (actual or remembered), or our own internal dialogue. Kinesthetic links could include the touches of friends, the feel of sand under our toes as we walk on the beach, the feel of the wind in our face, or the feel of a back massage. Olfactory/Gustatory links could include the smell of a special perfume or cologne, the smell of fresh-cut hay, the taste of a cool beverage, or the taste of a grilled steak. All of these stimuli or links can produce a highly predictable response from us.

As teachers, we link students daily through voice tones, words, gestures, facial expressions, and touches. Most of the time, we are unaware of the impact of our actions. We all carry with us a memory of a teacher from our school days who had a way of emphasizing a point so that it remains clear to us years later. How this teacher was able to impress this memory on us is an example of a powerful link. The teacher who flicks the room lights on and off to get the attention of his class is using a visual link. The teacher who claps his hands to get the attention of his class is using an auditory link, as is the teacher who clears his throat as an indication that he wants to speak.

Unfortunately, not all links that students experience are positive. Students may have early negative experiences in particular subjects. A link may be established. Every time a negative experience occurs in conjunction with that particular subject, the link is more solidly established. If positive experiences do not counterbalance the negative experiences, then students will have negative perceptions of that subject and, in all probability, their achievement in that subject will be nil.

"Test anxiety" is another example of negative linking. Students may be very conscientious, bright and well prepared, but because of the establishment of previous negative links, they do not score well on tests because their minds "go blank."

Links need not be established over a long period of time to be powerful. Frequently, a person's original experience has the most impact in establishing a link. Other experiences can serve to reinforce that link. Links provide easy access to a particular representation (V, A, K or O), because all experiences are represented as sensory sets. When one part of that experience or sensory set is reinstated (for example, visual), the other parts of the sensory set (A, K and O) are always, to some degree, reinstated. While to some extent similar to the classical Stimulus-Response psychological theories, linking does not require constant reinforcement as does the classical S-R techniques.

One of the most common and intricate linking systems is our language. A word like "love" can be a link for internal representations that draw upon our previous sensory experiences. To understand the word "love" we need to access past experiences: visual, auditory, kinesthetic and olfactory, regarding the experiences with "love" that we have had. One possible experience follows:

Fig. 15: <u>Language As A Link</u>

V^e "Love"

V^i image of loved one

A^r sound of voice

K_r^i remember feelings of being touched

O_r^i remembered smell of perfume or cologne

The word "love" links a particular set of representations in each of us. If the word "love" was altered by adding the word "brotherly" to it, different representations would be accessed as each of us probably has different links for this term. Another language link would be a word like "success"; similar representations can be identified for that word.

Linking Procedures

Before learning to establish links in others, it will be helpful to learn to establish a link with yourself. The following exercise is designed for two people. One example of an easily established link is the "State of Excellence" link. Each person has many states of excellence. Select a state of excellence (confidence, or happiness, or positiveness), that you would like to duplicate at will. Step into an imaginary circle and physically demonstrate or model what your "state of excellence" looks like. Your partner takes a mental snapshot of how you look in your "state of excellence", and you make yourself aware of your stance, your body position, your entire physiology. Step back from the circle, select a "stuck" or undesirable state (depression, or confusion, or anger), but before you immerse yourself completely into the "stuck" state, your partner gently pulls you back into the circle and you resume your "state of excellence" posture. Your partner verifies that you have again achieved your desired state. This very potent link can assist anyone in maintaining a consistent posture of excellence, and it dramatically illustrates the interrelationship between physiological states and emotional states.

Links can be established to make you feel good even when circumstances are depressing, to motivate and stimulate you, to make you feel more creative, or to relax you. The following exercise, done alone, can be used to link a feeling of pleasantness and well-being. Select a part of your body such as your wrist, or upper arm, or shoulder, that is not often touched, but can be touched when you choose without awkwardness or embarrassment in public. Then, follow these directions:

1. Find a place where you can relax and not be disturbed. Let your mind drift back to a time when you were happy and felt very good.

   a. Recreate that experience in your mind's eye by mapping the situation. The map would incorporate the following:

      V^e -   Remember what you saw at the time.

      V^i -   Recall any internal images you experienced at the time.

      A^e -   Recall any sounds, voices or noises you heard.

      A^i -   Remember any internal dialogue there may have been.

      K^e -   If there were any external feelings, recall them.

      K^i -   Remember your internal feelings.

      O^e -   Recall any smells or tastes associated with this experience.

      O^i -   If any remembered smells or tastes were triggered by this experience, recall them.

   Each sensory system is checked out externally and internally to determine its impact and intensity in the experience.

2. Each time part of the sensory map triggers part of your experience, squeeze or press firmly that part of your body that you have chosen to link.

132

3. Now you have a link that can be triggered or activated whenever it is needed. To trigger or to activate your link, simply squeeze or press the area of your body where you did the linking. Those linked feelings will return magically. Now, test the link. To increase the power of the link, experiences can be "combined." See the section entitled "Combining Links" later in this chapter.

While linking can be used in a variety of ways, the linking procedure can be used to link resource states that the student wants or needs to access at any given time to meet a particular outcome. It is assumed that the steps leading up to the Remedial Frame have already been completed.

1. Direct the students to identify needed resources and complete one of the three following steps:

   a. ask the students to remember a time when they had those resources; then direct the students to form an image and step into that image; or

   b. if students have not experienced a time when they had the resources, then direct the students to picture someone that they know that exhibits the desired state and/or the resources. They should make the image into movie form and pretend to step into the image and have the experience; or

   c. if students have not had the experience and do not know anyone who has the desired experience, direct the students to imagine what it would be like to have the experience. They can make an image of themselves or another person having those resources and step into the picture;

   d. check to see that the selected step provides what is desired.

2. As the students access a, b, or c in Step 1, the students link the process. The link should be kinesthetic - a touch on a knee, hand, arm, or shoulder. To ensure a strong link, the designated place should be touched as the students experience their most intense feelings (one finger pressed firmly will do nicely).

3. Using the kinesthetic link, have the students "map" the experience for the desired state. "Mapping" the experience is accomplished by focusing the attention of the students on each part of the sensory system (V^e, V^i, A^e, A^i, K^e, K^i, O^e, O^i) just as was done in establishing a link for your pleasantness and well-being. Each time part of the map appears in the students' experience, the student should touch the spot previously selected for the kinesthetic link.

4. Direct the students to release the link, and test the situation by having the students mentally project into the future and put themselves in an upcoming situation when they think they will need their link. This process of projecting into the future is referred to as "future pacing." Observe the sensory feedback (facial expression, breathing, etc.) of the students as they activate their link. The students' sensory feedback should approach the state associated with their link. It may require a couple of minutes before the link creates the desired state change

133

Scenario to Illustrate Linking (T - teacher; S - student)

T: "Billy you said that it's really hard for you to get enthusiastic enough to do your math homework, so sometimes it doesn't get done and the rest of the time it's a real struggle to do it."

S: "Yeah, it sure is."

T: "You'd like to feel more like doing your math so it wouldn't be such a hassle for you."

S: "That's right!"

T: "I'm going to show you how you can help yourself have that feeling whenever you want to have it."

S: "Sounds good to me."

T: "I want you to select a spot on your body such as your wrist or elbow that is not touched very often by you or anyone else, and that can be conveniently touched when you want to feel motivated."

S: "I'll choose my left wrist."

T: "Fine. Can you remember a time when you were highly motivated to do something?"

S: "Yes. I had to do a science project last year and that was very interesting. It was entered in the science fair and I won an award."

T: "Terrific! I want you to remember a time when you really wanted to work on that project. (Pauses.) Do you now remember that time?"

S: "Yes." The teacher observes Billy's facial expression, breathing, gestures, eye movement pattern, etc. to verify that he is experiencing the situation.

T: "I'd like for you to make a picture of yourself in that experience, and then step into that picture."

S: "O.K."

T: "As I ask you some questions, each time that you recall something that relates to your experience, press your wrist with your other hand."

"If you are seeing something outside yourself like people, or things or animals, remember them and press your wrist." (Pause.)

"If you make some pictures inside your head during your experience, remember those pictures and press your wrist." (Pause.)

"If you heard voices or sounds during your experience remember them now and press your wrist." (Pause.)

"If you had an internal conversation with yourself during this experience, then remember what you said to yourself and press your wrist." (Pause.)

"If you felt any external feelings, such as the feel of your clothes touching your body or the feel of your body touching a chair, or the ground, press your wrist." (Pause.)

"Remember those feelings of motivation that you experienced and press your wrist." (Pause.)

"If there were any smells or tastes during your experience then remember them and press your wrist." (Pause.)

"Billy, I'd like to have you release your wrist. That was quite a trip, wasn't it?" (This interruption is a state break. A state break is a movement or statement that causes a change in the person's existing state.)

"Now I'd like you to press your wrist." (The teacher determines from the sensory feedback whether the link works.)

"I'd like to have you go into the future to a time when you feel the need to study your math." (The teacher observes the sensory feedback.)

"When you have reached that time, press your wrist."

"How well did that pressing work for you?" (The sensory feedback will indicate if the link works.)

S: "Wow! Unbelievable!"

T: "Great! When you know that you have a math assignment to do and the time is appropriate for you to begin work on it, press your spot so that you will feel motivated to complete your math assignment."

Alternatives

Alternative #1

If students have difficulty remembering a time when they have been motivated, the teacher can challenge them with appropriate questions and statements. "You can't remember any time that you ever felt that you really wanted to do something?" "Think hard, I'm sure you can remember a time that you wanted very much to do something."

Should the challenge not bring forth the desired experience, the teacher can use another approach.

T: "Each of us has many resources that we can draw upon. These resources can include feelings of persistence, or confidence, or strength, or decisiveness. What resources would help you to be motivated?"

S: "I don't know - I guess confidence, strength - those would be good."

T: "Excellent! Can you think of any other resources that would be helpful to have?"

135

S: "No."

(The teacher may suggest some additional resources if he feels it would be helpful to do so.)

T: "Billy, I'd like you to remember a time when you felt very confident, very strong, and very secure. Can you remember a time?"

S: "Yes."

T: "Billy, I want you to remember, in detail, that experience. When you can remember it very clearly, nod your head." (The teacher observes Billy's sensory feedback to verify that he is accessing the experience.)

"I'd like you to make a picture of yourself in that experience and then step into that picture."

The scenario continues as in the original example.

Alternative #2

If students cannot remember one particular time when they felt confident, strong and had desire, then follow this scenario.

T: "Billy, can you remember a time when you felt confident?"

S: "Yes."

(The teacher follows the procedures through the mapping of the experiences. Then the teacher returns to the other two resources and asks students to remember powerful, but separate experiences when they felt strength and desire. These experiences are mapped and the exercise is followed to its conclusion.)

Alternative #3

T: "Billy, have you had a time when you really felt like doing something?"

S: "No."

(The teacher challenges Billy to be certain this is the case.)

T: "Do you know someone or have you seen someone who you think is motivated?"

S: "Yes."

T: "All right, I'd like to have you imagine that person in a situation being motivated. Can you see them (or if the person is auditory, "hear" them)? O.K. Now make that picture and have the experience."

(The teacher continues through the rest of the steps. This scenario can also be followed for each of the other resources - confidence and strength.)

Alternative #4

T: "Billy, have you had a time when you experienced feelings of really wanting to accomplish a task or to do something, or go somewhere?"

S: "No. I can't remember any."

T: "None at all?"

S: "No."

T: "I would like to have you imagine how you would feel, how you would look, and what you would say for yourself, if you had that feeling. Can you do that?"

S: "I think so."

T: "Then take your time and make the picture of yourself and/or hear yourself experiencing those feelings."

(The teacher continues through the remainder of the exercise. The same scenario can be repeated for each of the other resources - confidence and strength.)

Combining Links

Should a single link fail to achieve the desired outcome, links can be "combined." Combining links means that subjects remember several powerful experiences associated with the resources they seek. These experiences are individually linked in the same manner and in the same place. For example, if a kinesthetic link (a spot on the knee) has been used, each experience will be linked on that same spot. In this manner a very powerful link can be established. Links are combined in the same manner that single links are created.

Scenario To Illustrate Combining Links

"Future pacing" means asking subjects to project into the future to create or imagine a situation when they would need the state created by a link. After observing the future pacing in the "Billy case," the teacher believes that the sensory feedback indicates the linking technique is unsuccessful. He decides to use the combining link technique to provide a stronger link.

T: "Billy, I want you to think of the same experience as before when you felt highly motivated to do something."

S: "O.K."

(The teacher observes the sensory feedback to determine that the experience is being recalled, and he follows through the rest of the procedures.)

T: "Billy, I want you to select another powerful experience when you really wanted to go somewhere or do something. Can you remember another one?"

S: "Yes."

(The teacher continues through the exercise. He may wish to recreate several more experiences to make a very powerful link. He may also wish to have Billy select experiences that incorporate the confidence and strength resources he originally sought.)

Remember, links can be kinesthetic, visual, auditory, or a combination of the three. Examples of kinesthetic links were evident in these scenarios. Visual links could include gestures and facial expressions. Auditory links would include particular voice tones and/or words. The most powerful links would be a combination of V, A, and K links. A particular touch could be used in conjunction with certain voice tones and facial expressions or gestures.

Integrating Links

If the combining link technique does not seem to work, then Integrating Links will be a more powerful choice. Integrating Links simply means that the present state and the desired state are separately linked. Both links are then activated simultaneously, and the two responses are integrated. After the links are integrated, the student will have more possible ways to automatically respond to present state stimuli. To integrate links effectively, the links must be of equal intensity. Therefore, it may be necessary to combine links for the desired state, to offset the powerful effects of the present or negative state link. (Steps for Integrating Links can be found on pages 141-142, 228 and ·229.)

Scenario To Illustrate Integrating Links

A detailed discussion of the objectives and technique for each step follows the Scenario.

Step 1

T: "Sarah, you told me that you would like to feel calm, cool and collected when you take an exam. Is that correct?"

S: "Yes!"

T: "It is helpful as we go through this process to give a label to the feelings that occur when you take a test. This label could be a name, a nickname, or whatever you would like to call them."

S: "I'd like to call them 'Panic'."

Step 2

T: "Fine. I'd like you to imagine that you are taking a test and that you are feeling those negative feelings that normally occur in that instance."

(Go through the experience map and establish a link with voice tones and a gesture. The gesture can be whatever seems natural to you or to the student. Sometimes students will make a particular gesture when talking about the negative stimulus. If they do, then use that gesture as a link for the negative state. I suggest using a kinesthetic (K) link for the positive experience because a K link is very potent. If a K link is used as a present state link, it can overwhelm any visual and/or tonal links that are being used for the positive experience(s). However, there may be times when you wish to use a present state link.)

138

Step 3

Then do a state break by making a comment or movement and continue.

T: "Has there ever been a time when you took a test that you felt calm, cool and collected?"

S: "No."

T: "You never had a single test experience where you felt relaxed?"

S: "I can't remember any."

(If the student had remembered a situation, the teacher could have used a K link and sought to combine links to develop a strong positive link. Since the student couldn't remember a time during a test that he felt relaxed, the teacher tried a different approach.)

Step 4

T: "Can you think of any internal resources that would be helpful in overcoming 'Panic'?"

S: "Confidence would be helpful. Organization would be too. Relaxation. and maybe flexibility."

T: "Are there any other resources that you think would be helpful?"

S: "I don't think so."

Step 5

T: "Has there ever been a time when you really felt confident, organized, relaxed and flexible?"

(If the student cannot find an all-encompassing experience, then the teacher can help the student chunk down to a single experience for each resource. Each experience would need to be mapped and linked. After all experiences were linked, the teacher would continue to the state break and complete the exercise.)

S: "Let me think. Yes I can think of a good one!"

T: "As we go through this experience together I am going to lightly touch you on the shoulder when I sense that you remember experiencing something. O.K.?"

S: "O.K."

(The teacher goes through the mapping process lightly squeezing or touching the shoulder or arm or hand or knee each time the student has an experience in that particular sensory system.)

Step 6

The teacher breaks the state, and then continues.

Step 7

T: "Sarah, let's see what happens when I make this gesture." (The teacher makes the same gesture that he used to link the present state experience. He also makes the statement using the same voice tones as he did to link the present state. He observes the sensory feedback of the present or "stuck state" link.)

Step 8

Assuming the sensory feedback indicates that the present state link is working, the teacher breaks the state.

Step 9

T: "How are you feeling now?" (Presses shoulder link.) (A change of state can sometimes take one or two minutes before sensory feedback indicates the change, so be patient. Increasing the pressure on the link may be helpful.)

Step 10

The teacher breaks the state.

Step 11

The teacher then activates both links, integrating them.

Step 12

After observing the integration process and its completion, the teacher again breaks the state.

Step 13

T: "Let's see, Sarah, what happens now."

(The teacher activates the old present state link with gestures and observes the sensory feedback. There should be minimal, if any, feedback.)

If there is relatively strong present state feedback, then return to Step 4, create more resources, develop a stronger desired state link and progress through the remaining steps.

Step 14

T: "Sarah, let's go into the future to the next time when you expect you will have an exam. Be there, see what you would normally see, hear the normal sounds that you will hear, and tell me how you feel now."

S: "Gee, that's weird. I don't feel those bad feelings any more!"

T: "Great!"

For maximum transfer, do two more future pacing situations.

Steps For Integrating Links

Now let's look at the steps in detail. The steps for Integrating Links are as follows:

1)   Identify the automatic response, or the present state.

Ask the students to label it. The label can be a nickname, a number, a letter, a color, etc. The use of a label makes it easier to describe the present state situation or the response.

2)   Direct the students to access the state. The teacher links it and creates the sensory set map (see p. 132). As students match their experience with the sensory map, the teacher reinforces the link for each sensory system that was part of the students' present state experience. For example, if students had been linked kinesthetically in the present state, the teacher releases the link. Then as the students are led through the mapping procedure, every time they are aware of accessing one of the sensory systems, the teacher lightly touches the same kinesthetic link.

3)   When the mapping procedure has been completed, a state break (something that causes a change in the person's existing state) should be enacted. The purpose of this state break is to separate the students from their present state. This state break can easily be accomplished by asking the students a question about something else, commenting on their clothes or hair style or jewelry. A sensory check of the students will indicate if the state break is successful.

4)   The students should identify the resources that they need to attain their desired state.

5)   The students should access the desired state and be linked in it. (Remember to use a different link!) Utilize the sensory set mapping procedure and, again, reinforce the link each time it is necessary.

6)   At this point, employ another state break to separate the students from the desired state.

7)   Test the present state link by activating it and observing the sensory activity of the students to see if the link is functioning.

8)   Break the state.

9)   Test the desired state link and observe the sensory activity of the students to see if the link is functioning.

10)   Break the state.

11)   Activate both links simultaneously, and wait for the integration to occur. Sensory feedback will indicate when the integration occurs. There is often a rapid shifting between the two states, followed by a look of confusion on the

students' faces. When this confusion occurs, I sometimes find it helpful to deactivate the present state link and to continue activating the desired state link thus reinforcing the desired state. I also make positive and appropriate comments about the outcome being achieved.

12) When the integration process is over, <u>break the state.</u>

13) <u>Test the present state link</u> by activating it. The students' sensory feedback should indicate that the present state feelings are not as strong as they once were.

14) A final test is to <u>have the students future pace.</u> Sensory observation will indicate the success of the intervention.

15) If the integrating links technique has not worked, it may help to add to the desired state by combining links. In that case, go back to #4 and help the students recall, access and build several desired state situations. This procedure will be more likely to offset the powerful present state stimulus.

The Thirty Second Integrating Link

The Thirty Second Integrating Link Technique is a simplified method of the formalized linking process that can integrate links very effectively. If the teacher observes a student having difficulty and the integrating link intervention seems to be in order, the teacher can quietly walk over to the student and say something like, "It looks as though you're having a hard time of it." Once the student's feedback confirms the teacher's statement, the teacher says, "Sally, how would you like to be feeling?" Sally replies that she'd like to feel "less anxious." The teacher asks if feeling "less anxious" means she'd like to "feel calm." Sally says "Yes." The teacher asks, "Sally, have you ever had a time in your life when you felt calm and relaxed?" She nods her head affirmatively. The teacher says, "I want you to remember that time; what you saw (pause), what you heard (pause), what you felt (pause), anything that you can recall that makes it seem real." When the teacher is satisfied that the student is accessing the positive experience, he links the experience by touching the student's shoulder, or elbow.

The teacher, still maintaining the link and increasing the pressure slightly, has the student access the present or negative state. An integrating of links will occur, provided the positive link is equal in strength to the present state link. If necessary, more positive links could be combined and then integrated.

The Two-Handed Link

The Two-Handed Link is an effective tool to use in assisting students to make good decisions. The teacher extends either the right hand or the left out in front, and to one side of himself. Looking intently at that hand, the teacher could say, "Tim, you have this choice. You can do _____ and _____, and probably _____ will occur as a result." Establish a rhythmic movement with each hand as the link is accessed. Still keeping the first hand extended, the teacher then extends the other hand in the opposite direction, and says, "On the other hand, you have this choice". The teacher describes the choice(s). (The teacher is holding the two hands out to either side; the student now has two choices.) If it is evident to the teacher which choice would be best for the student, the teacher can say, "I know you'll make the right choice," and the teacher then moves the hand identified with the favorable choice toward the student. The student will then have a strong unconscious desire to carry out that particular choice.

The Visual Scramble

The Visual Scramble is a two-handed link that can be used to integrate new ideas and behaviors. The same format is used, and once the hands become links, they are slowly brought together and the fingers are interlaced. What occurs on the unconscious level is an integration of links. For example, suppose a student has all the information and steps needed to solve a particular math problem, but a lack of understanding prevents him from integrating the information and steps and solving the problem. The teacher could extend one hand and say, "Jim, you have this information _____ and these steps _____." Again, the teacher describes this information and the steps. As the teacher clasps his hands together, he states, "Won't it be a relief to you when all of this information and these steps jell in your mind so that you will be able to solve this problem?" An integration of the two sets of information and steps described by the teacher will occur on an unconscious level with the student. These procedures will provide the student with some power-packed unconscious resources to better resolve the math problem.

The Visual Scramble can also be helpful in dealing with behavior problems. One hand can be the present state, the other hand can be the desired state. As they are clasped, the teacher can, in a positive, enthusiastic tone say, "Let's save the things you do that are right and put these new things with it and see if you don't have fewer problems."

Should Integrating Links not create the desired change, it will probably be necessary to utilize the Transforming Technique, which is explained in the following chapter.

Five conditions are necessary to establish links:

1) the unusualness of the stimulus. Links can be visual, auditory, kinesthetic, olfactory/gustatory, or some combination of those four. (For our purposes only the establishment of V, A, and K links will be discussed.) An example of a visual link could be the use of one or more appropriate gestures. Examples of auditory links could be a noise, a voice tone, or a word or a combination of them. Kinesthetic links involve touching part of the body. The uniqueness of the stimulus means that unusual, but appropriate gestures, noises, voice tones, words, or touches are more effective in establishing a link than are more conventional gestures, noises, voices, voice tones, words or touch links. A kinesthetic link established on a person's ear lobe, rather than on a knee, would be more effective because the ear lobe is less frequently touched in day-to-day activity than is the knee.

2) the singularity of the response. If, for example, a teacher is linking "confidence" in a student, that feeling of confidence should not be unduly contaminated by other feelings, because the link will reactivate not only the feeling of confidence but the other feelings as well. The teacher should use appropriate questions to fine tune the desired state (e.g. confidence) in a student to the exclusion of the other feelings that may be present. Through sensory observation of the student, the teacher will be more certain that he is linking a pure response and potential contamination problems will be overcome or eliminated.

143

3) the intensity of the response. The greater the intensity of the response, the more effective the link will be. For that reason, the response, if possible, should include the entire sensory set (V, A, K and O/G). In addition, the response should be as vivid as the student can remember. Just how to develop the sensory set to its maximum has already been discussed on page 132.

4) appropriate timing. For effective linking to occur, the response needs to be linked just as it reaches its peak. Ask students to experience the response before linking. Sensory observation will indicate when the response begins to peak. Directing the student to reactivate the response a second time and, then, linking it at its peak will strengthen the link.

5) the environmental factor. Any link needs to fit into the students' environmental system. The development of a well-formed outcome, which includes the advantages and the disadvantages of the new outcome, plus the inclusion of Steps 1-4, should ensure a desirable environmental fit.

The length of time a link will be effective is dependent upon the uniqueness of the stimulus and how long the response remains useful to the person.

Revising Life Patterns

Revising Life Patterns alters the effects of a particular link - or response to a stimulus - that students have had for some time. An example of such a response could be a negative attitude toward a particular subject where students either frequently have negative experiences or block out the counterbalancing positive or neutral experiences and only remember the negative ones. Revising Life Patterns is an integrating links technique in that it enables students to go back to deal with the origin of their response and subsequent times when the same response has been generated throughout a portion of their life. The steps in Revising Life Patterns are as follows:

1) Kinesthetically link the student's negative state (present state response), and then release the link. The exception to these directions would be to hold this link if the student has trouble remembering other examples of this state as asked for in Step 2.)

2) Tell the student to drift back in time, remembering other times when he had the same response, and tell him to remember the first time the response occurred. Have the student nod his head to indicate each time the response occurred. Using the same K link, lightly tap that spot to link each response.

3) Establish a new positive link by holding the student's hand. Ask the student: "If you knew then what you know now, what additional choices or resources could you have used?" Squeeze the hand each time a choice or a resource is mentioned.

4) Still holding the hand link, ask the student to make a picture of that younger person that was him. Direct the student to tell that younger person what would have been helpful for him to know so that he could have felt and/or acted differently.

5) Direct the student to return to the earliest time that he can remember experiencing the negative response. Next, ask him to remember each experience from the earliest instance to the most recent. As the student accesses each experience, ask him to nod his head. Integrate links by

144

squeezing the hand link while lightly tapping the negative link.

6) <u>Release all links and have the student mentally go to the next time that the response could develop.</u> To determine the success of this technique, observe the student's sensory feedback. The sensory feedback should reflect either an absence of negative state feedback, or it should reflect aspects of the positive link. (Simplified steps for Revising Life Patterns can be found on pg.230.)

Scenario To Illustrate Revising Life Patterns

T: "Helen, you indicated that you've had feelings of anxiety every time that you've taken a test for as long as you remember. Is that correct?"

S: "Yes."

T: "You've also indicated that you want to feel relaxed and confident when you take tests."

S: "Yes."

T: "To assist you in being more relaxed during a test, I will need to touch your arm and to hold your hand."

S: "O.K."

T: "If it should bother you at any time, please tell me; however it's essential to the success of what I want to do, to be able to touch your arm and to hold your hand."

(As he goes through the sensory map, the teacher establishes a K link for the present state response by touching the student's arm. The link is then released.)

T: "Helen, I'd like to have you drift back in time and remember other times when you have had that feeling of anxiety when taking tests. Each time you remember one of those times, nod your head."

(The teacher links each situation by lightly tapping the present state K link. After the linking is finished, the teacher holds the student's hand.)

T: "What resources would be helpful for you to have in order to be able to achieve your outcome?"

(If necessary, explain and give examples.)

S: "Well, I think that having confidence, being relaxed, and being able to remember the material would be really helpful resources to have."

(The teacher gently squeezes the student's hand each time a resource is mentioned. The teacher continues to hold the hand link.)

T: "Helen, I'd like you to make an image or picture of that younger person that you were when you experienced this anxiety, and tell that younger person what it is that they needed to know so that they wouldn't have had to feel or act that way."

(The teacher gives the student ample time to achieve this undertaking.)

T: "Now, Helen, I'd like to have you return to the first time that you remember experiencing those undesirable feelings and then remember the last time you felt that way. As you remember each experience, nod your head."

(As the student accesses each experience, the teacher integrates links by squeezing the hand link while lightly tapping the negative link. The teacher then releases all links.)

T: "O.K., Helen. Now I'd like to have you imagine the next time that you know that you will have a test. Hear what you would hear, see what you would see, and feel what you now feel."

(The teacher observes sensory feedback to determine the success of the Revising Life Patterns Technique.)

Disassociation

As the term indicates, the disassociation technique can be used to prevent students from experiencing strong feelings that they wish to avoid. In this sense, students can "disassociate" from the feelings and can more readily cope with life. The steps are as follows:

1)   Help students determine a positive outcome.

2)   Ask students to select a neutral or disassociated situation and link it kinesthetically. A disassociated situation is a neutral situation that has little internal kinesthetic feeling associated with it. This could be as simple an experience as walking down the street.

3)   Ask students to recall the "stuck state" or present state situation.

4)   "Pop" students out of the stuck state with the neutral or disassociated link. The link should be held until sensory feedback indicates that disassociation has occurred.

5)   Direct students to select resources that would be helpful to them in neutralizing or disassociating from the stuck situation. Link the resources using the same link as was used for the disassociated or neutral state.

6)   Ask students to recall the stuck state and integrate the disassociated link.

7)   Observe the students' sensory feedback to determine if the disassociation technique was successful. (Simplified steps for Disassociation can be found on pg. 231.)

A number of sensory cues indicate when students are experiencing disassociation:

   a)   shallow breathing high in the chest
   b)   eyes above center
   c)   face mobile
   d)   no body movement
   e)   head tilted slightly back
   f)   shoulders back.

Scenario To Illustrate Disassociation

The student has expressed feelings of fear when interacting with a particular teacher.

T: "Tim, if I correctly understand your outcome, you would like to have feelings of coolness and calmness when you have anything to do with Mr. Thomas."

S: "Yes, I certainly would!"

T: "I'd like you to think of a time when you were doing something that you had few feelings about - something kind of neutral, such as walking down the street or lying in the sun. Can you remember such a time?"

S: "Yes."

(The teacher links the neutral or disassociated experience. Probably a kinesthetic link would be most desirable.)

T: "Tim, I'd like to have you recall the last experience you had with Mr. Thomas."

(By gauging the sensory feedback of the student, the teacher will be able to tell when the student is in the stuck situation. The teacher then "pops" the student out of the negative state by activating the neutral link. Sensory feedback will indicate when this is accomplished.)

T: "Tim, what resources would be helpful to you to achieve your outcome of feeling cool and calm when you are with Mr. Thomas?"

S: "Being able to relax would certainly help. I wish I could laugh more and feel strong."

(The teacher links the resources using the same link that was used for the disassociated or neutral state.)

T: "Tim, I'd like you once again to recall the last time that you met with Mr. Thomas."

(The teacher observes the student's sensory feedback and then activates the link, thereby integrating the disassociated anchor. Sensory feedback indicates the success of the disassociation. The teacher could give instructions for future pacing. The "acid" test will, of course, be the next meeting with Mr. Thomas.)

Applying Remedial Techniques To The Elementary Student

Learn to establish positive links with your students. When they are feeling happy, joyful, successful, etc., observe their entry cues and when they are at a peak moment, link the feeling with a smile, a nod, a wink, a touch, a word, a tone, or a combination of these. Make the link reproducible, and use it to retrieve the feeling when it would be advantageous for the student to have that positive feeling. Teach students to establish their own links and to use them periodically. If necessary, combining links can be a part of the process.

The Integrating Link Technique can be used with elementary students in several different ways. If students' own individual links are powerful and contain resources that match those in their outcome, the teacher can direct them into their stuck state and activate their own link. This action will result in integrating links. Students would then have to develop a new individual link to serve the same function as the old one. Another suggestion is for the teacher to activate his own positive link for a particular student when that student is in a stuck state. If the teacher's link for the student is strong enough, integrating links can result. (The teacher would then need to establish a new link for that student.) The Thirty Second Integrating Link Technique can be an appropriate, easy and successful maneuver to use in some situations.

If necessary, the formal Integrating Link Technique can be slightly modified for use with elementary students, primarily by simplifying the language and the process. In this way, it can be speeded up. The process will be completed more rapidly after it has been practiced several times. The Revising Life Patterns Technique and the Disassociation Technique are probably best used in their present form.

Exercise #40
Reinforcing Actions Or Words

Purpose: To learn to use links to reinforce selected actions.

'A' leaves the group.

'B' is to reinforce a particular action or set of words of 'A's, either through positive or negative reinforcement. ('B' may choose to wait and select one of 'A's actions or words after 'A' starts conversing.) An example of a positive strategy would be to smile, or to nod one's head, or to tilt one's posture forward, etc. to reinforce a particular movement or word. Negative reinforcement could imply laughing inappropriately, using disrupting tactics, frowning, etc. to reinforce a particular movement or word.

'C' observes, judges and referees.

Rotate the roles.

Collateral Exercise #40 and #41

Purpose: To learn to use links to reinforce selected student behavior.

The teacher selects a student and chooses a behavior that he would like to reinforce.

Using one or more links, the teacher reinforces the behavior.

Exercise #41
Shaping Behavior

Purpose: To learn to use links to shape behavior.

'A' leaves the room or moves out of hearing range of the group.

'B' identifies how he will shape 'A's behavior in some way (e.g.: getting 'A' to tilt his head to the right or to the left, etc.). 'B' then recalls 'A' and carries on a conversation with 'A', while shaping his behavior.

'C' observes and determines if the shaping technique has worked.

Rotate the roles.

Exercise #42
Establishing An Individual Link

Purpose: To learn to establish a link.

Select a particular state that you would like to be able to access. Use the same linking technique as the one on page 132, or if the state is appropriate use the State of Excellence link. Test the link to be certain that it works.

Exercise #43 - Assisting Students
In Establishing Their Individual Link

Purpose: To help students establish a link.

Using the same technique as described on pages 132-133, help a student develop a positive link of his choosing. Have the student test the link.

Exercise #44
Combining Links

Purpose: To learn to Combine Links.

'A' selects a state that he wishes to change by combining links.

(Continued)

Collateral Exercises #42, #43 and #44

Purpose: To assist students in developing links.

The teacher chooses a student and assists him in developing a link.

If necessary, the teacher helps the student combine links.

Exercise #44
Combining Links
(Continued)

'B' completes the necessary steps prior to the actual combining links technique and then assists 'A' through the combining links procedure.

'C' observes.

Rotate the roles.

Exercise #45
Integrating Links

Purpose: To learn to Integrate Links.

'A' selects a response that he wishes to change that is suitable for use with an integrating links technique.

'B' completes the necessary steps prior to using the integrating links technique and then takes 'A' through the technique.

'C' observes.

Rotate the roles.

Collateral Exercise #45

Purpose: To execute the Integrating Links technique with a student.

The teacher selects a student with a response that is suitable for the integrating links procedure. He executes the integrating links procedure.

Exercise #46
Revising Life Patterns

Purpose: To learn to use the Revising Life Patterns technique.

'A' selects a suitable response for the revising life patterns technique.

'B' completes the necessary steps prior to the revising life patterns technique and guides 'A' through the technique.

'C' observes.

Rotate the roles.

Collateral Exercise #46

Purpose: To use the Revising Life Patterns Technique with a student.

The teacher selects a student with a problem suitable for the revising life patterns technique and uses the technique.

150

Exercise #47
Disassociation From a "Stuck" State

Purpose: To learn to neutralize a "stuck" state. (A stuck state is a negative state in which an individual lacks the resources, or the knowledge to change his state to a more positive one.)

Phase I

'A' chooses a stuck state that he has previously experienced and imagines himself in that state.

'B' helps 'A' to know what the stuck state is by describing what he sees, by getting 'A' to feel his posture, etc.

'C' observes.

Phase II

'B' moves 'A' out of the spot in which he was standing, and twirls around or otherwise disassociates 'A' from that state.

'A' tells 'B' what 'A' now sees and feels, i.e.: how he is different than when he is in the stuck state.

'C' determines that 'A' has indeed left his stuck state.

Rotate the roles.

Exercise #48
Overcoming Stuck States

Purpose: To learn to overcome stuck states.

Phase I

'A' accesses a helpful behavior that he could use when he is in a particular stuck state. 'A' then visualizes a picture of himself portraying that behavior.

(Continued)

Collateral Exercises #47 and #49

Purpose: To use the Disassociation Technique with a student.

The teacher selects a student who wishes to disassociate from some intense feelings, and uses the disassociation technique.

Collateral Exercise #48

Purpose: To help a student overcome a stuck state.

The teacher chooses a student who is having difficulty overcoming a "stuck" state.

(Continued)

'A' then accesses the stuck state and he recalls the mental image of his helpful behavior and superimposes that on his stuck state physiology. If the mental image of his new behavior looks O.K., 'A' then steps into the picture and has the new experience.

'B' helps 'A' overcome the stuck state by describing what he or she sees.

'C' observes.

Phase II

'A' selects a model of the same sex as himself and visualizes how that person would have handled the previously chosen stuck situation. 'A' steps into the visualization and then steps into the stuck state and pretends that he is that person handling his stuck state.

'B' describes to 'A' what he observes about 'A's change of behavior.

'C' observes.

Phase III

'A' selects a model from the opposite sex and follows the same directions as in Phase II.

'B' and 'C' also follow the same directions.

Rotate the roles.

He has the student select a helpful behavior that he could use in a particular stuck state. The student assumes the stuck state, recalls the mental image of his helpful behavior and superimposes that image on his stuck state physiology. If the mental image of the new behavior looks O.K., the student steps into the picture and has the new experience.

Next, the student selects a model of the same sex and visualizes how that person would have handled the previously chosen stuck situation. The student steps into the visualization and then steps into the stuck state and pretends that he is that person handling his stuck state.

Next, the student selects a model from the opposite sex and follows the direction in the previous paragraph.

Exercise #49
Disassociation

Purpose: To learn the Disassociation Technique.

'A' selects a situation where a disassociation response would be helpful.

'B' completes the necessary steps prior to the technique, and then guides 'A' through the technique.

'C' observes.

Rotate the roles.

Linking and the Classroom

Here are ten additional practical ways of establishing links in the classroom.

1) Establish link points (either using room location, posture, or other links) with chronic talkers to bring them back on task.

2) Establish one place from which all directions are given.

3) Create a quiet place where a student may voluntarily go when over-stimulated.

4) Create your own link to access particular states, such as relaxation, that would be helpful for you to have.

5) Link individual students and/or the entire class to relieve or prevent test anxiety.

6) Establish a location in the room that is used for solving problems.

7) Use a visual link (such as a cartoon character) to illustrate your mood at the beginning of each day.

8) Develop various visual links (3 or 4 gestures) and several auditory links (noises, voice tones, words, or combinations of these) to use when appropriate.

9) Establish a link point where new material is presented.

10) Teach students to create a link for themselves.

Summary

Remedial techniques (linking, combining links, integrating links, revising life patterns, and disassociation) are designed to give a student exhibiting a highly predictable behavior pattern to a particular stimulus, more response options. These options could include developing more positive responses to such feelings as test anxiety and negative attitudes, as well as changing a response that has been part of students' life patterns for a long period of time, and disassociating from the feelings caused by a particular stimulus. These techniques and those mentioned in the next chapter are very powerful. Use them with love and respect, and the pupil growth that you will witness will be truly astounding!

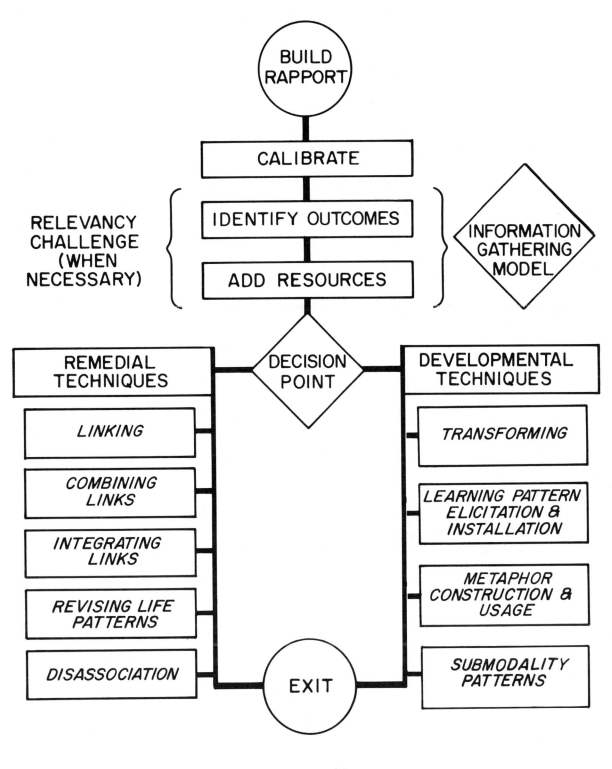

Chapter 17

DEVELOPMENTAL TECHNIQUES

A college student once asked me if I could help her with a problem related to studying. She was enrolled in a chemistry course which she needed for her major, but she was either oversleeping and missed the class or she would arrive late in a disorganized state. Ultimately, she knew her behavior was going to affect her grade in the course, and she wanted to change her behavior before her grade dropped. Her outcome was to resolve the conflict within herself so that she could regenerate and refocus her scholastic efforts and do well in the course. Since secondary gain appeared to be involved in this situation (she continued her behavior even though part of her knew it was not in her best interests), I chose to use the Transforming Technique. With the use of this technique conflicts between internal parts are resolved. In this instance, the conflict was between part of her that was concerned with her health and part of her that was concerned with her studies. The health part sought to have her take care of herself by receiving the sleep that she thought was necessary to her well-being. The academic part wanted her to succeed even if it cost her some sleep. The dilemma was interesting because whatever action the student took was bound to upset one of her parts. The Transforming Techniques helped her create some additional ways to meet the needs of the parts, so that she was able to realize her academic goals and she was able to get an adequate amount of sleep. A third person in the same class verified that after her session with me, she came to class on time and was organized. The student was able to change her behavior as a result of one fifteen minute meeting with me.

What student responses indicate the need for "Developmental Techniques?" What are "Developmental Techniques" and how are they utilized?

Developmental Techniques are applied to situations where a specific outcome is sought in one or more contexts (situations). These situations could include responses to stimuli that had existed throughout much of the student's academic life, such as long-term test anxiety, poor motivation, poor attitude toward school, underachievement, and unworkable or nonexistent subject matter learning patterns.

The four major **Developmental Techniques** include:

1) **Transforming**
2) **Learning Pattern Elicitation**
3) **Learning Pattern Installation**[4]
4) **Use of metaphors.**[5]
5) **Submodality Patterns**[6]

Before these techniques are administered, it is necessary to complete the steps from Building Rapport through the Decision Point.

Transforming

Transforming can change students' responses to an existing experience that involves a secondary gain. Not only do students exhibit undesirable behavior and realize that behavior is not to their advantage, but they gain something from the behavior. This

---

[4]Additional learning patterns is the subject of Chapter 19.
[5]Metaphor construction and usage is the subject of Chapter 20.
[6]Submodality Patterns is the subject of Chapter 21.

gain may be entirely unconscious, but it is difficult for them to change. This description could include such behaviors as lack of motivation, any undesirable responses continuing over a long period of time, and behavior indicating difficulties with controlling habits and behavior resulting in drug or substance abuse. Secondary gain would also include students frequently exhibiting psychosomatic symptoms.

Single-Sentence Transforming

One type of Transforming is the "Single-Sentence Transformer." The Single-Sentence Transformer can be used to change the meaning attached to a particular stimulus. In this instance the stimulus is acceptable, but the response is not. For example, students may say, "Gee, this work is hard!", or "I'm afraid of failing." (To see how a Single-Sentence Transformer changes the meaning of that statement, look at the "Meaning Transformation" column.) The Single-Sentence Transformer is also used to do "context" transformation. Context transformation means that as a result of the teacher's statement, particular students' responses are tied to a different set of circumstances or situations. Context transformation can lead to students changing their perspective on a matter. Changes in perspective may lead to behavioral changes. (For examples of context transformation, look at the "Context Transformation" column.) New perspectives brought about by Single-Sentence Transformation can cause a student to reevaluate his situation and can bring about surprising and rapid change.

Meaning Transformation	Context Transformation
S: "Gee, this work is hard."	S: "Gee, this work is hard."
T: "Yes, it is, but you'll learn a great deal and have a lot of personal satisfaction after working so hard and completing such a difficult assignment."	T: "Yes it is. Can you remember a time from your experience when you worked hard and found that it paid off for you?"
S: "I'm afraid of failing."	S: "I'm afraid of failing."
T: "I understand what you are saying. Someone once said that, "Fear is an invitation to learn."	T: "I understand what you are saying. Has there ever been a time in your experience when your fear of failing caused you to master something or to become successful in some way?"
S: "I never do anything right!"	S: "I never do anything right!"
T: "I can appreciate your feeling. Success frequently comes just when things seem futile."	T: "I can appreciate your feeling. Can you remember a situation where you had the same feelings, but somehow in the end you were successful?"

The Transforming Steps

If the various types of linking are unsuccessful in altering students' behavior, then secondary gain may be involved and the Transforming Technique should be used. The nine following steps illustrate the transformation process:

1) Students should identify and state in a positive form the behavior they want to change. Direct students to give their internal part that is causing the behavior, a label. The label can be a letter, or a number, or a color, or a nickname.

    If students have difficulty understanding what is meant by a "part", the teacher can use one of several approaches to explain this concept. If at all possible, use the students' model of the world to explain the concept. The concept could be explained in the sense that certain parts are responsible for executing various body functions: heart beat, blood pressure, etc. If students are athletic, relate the explanation to the fact that they perform athletic skills without always being consciously aware of their behavior. If they are old enough to drive a car, they perform unconscious behaviors. Once that understanding is developed, the teacher can say, "That's what I mean by "part," that unconscious motivator."

2) Ask students to focus inward and silently ask themselves if the part of them that is causing the behavior (use label), is willing to communicate. It may be helpful to explain that the part may choose to make contact in one of several ways: they may hear an internal voice; a color may appear in the mind's eye; a finger may twitch, or a feeling may develop. If there are no observable sensory signals, ask the students if they are getting any response.

    If there appears to be a sensory signal, ask the students to intensify the strength of the signal and confirm that the sensory signal is the one that they are seeking. If for any reason the part does not communicate, direct the students to ask the part why it does not wish to communicate. This procedure is usually enough of a stimulus to open communication and the sensory signal can then be determined.

    If the student's sensory signal is not auditory, instruct the student to make a visual image from their sensory signal. Direct questions can then be asked and sometimes direct answers will be forthcoming that greatly simplify this procedure.

3) Ask the students to thank the part for you and if possible direct them to thank it themselves for the behavior it has been producing. Thanking the part assumes that there has been a positive intent to its action even though the behavior may appear negative.

4) Direct the student to ask the part what it has been trying to do for them. If a negative answer should be forthcoming, for example, "to hurt myself," then the students are to ask what its positive intent was in wanting to "hurt themselves." (If there should be no response after trying several times - this is rare - then one option would be to continue through the remaining steps as though everything was proceeding as planned.

158

Should a lack of response arise, indicate to the students not to be concerned; this information is being given to them unconsciously.)

5) <u>Ask the students to contact their creative part, and ask it to come up with at least three new choices to satisify the positive intention of the original part.</u> If the students have any trouble in identifying the creative part, ask them if there <u>ever</u> was a time when they were creative. The answer should be affirmative and the students can be told that that is their creative part. If the students still have difficulty identifying the creative part, it is possible to "build" one. Asking the students questions about their activities will build a creative part. "Have you ever done anything out of the ordinary or anything different? Tell me about it." Conversation of this nature will frequently lead to experiences where creativity flourished. The teacher can help students understand that their creative part made the different experience a success and that this part should now be contacted.

In rare cases, when several attempts to elicit new alternatives seems to be failing, try one of these responses:

a. "Guess what the alternatives might be."

b. "If you did know the alternatives, what would they be?"

c. "Tonight I want you to dream the alternatives and tell me tomorrow."

d. "Remember someone who behaves effectively in this situation. What does that person do?"

6) <u>Direct the students to ask the original part if it will accept these new choices and implement them.</u> If there is an objection, have the students ask the part why it is objecting. It may be necessary to backtrack to Step 5 to obtain more choices. If there has been a lack of communication from the original part and if that continues, then tell the students that these new alternatives are being processed on an unconscious basis, and they will work just as well, if not better, as if they were being processed consciously. This time is opportune for a good voice link, such as a lowering of the voice, which serves as a signal to the student that now is the time to process and integrate the information unconsciously.

7) <u>Instruct the students to ask if any other parts object to the new choices.</u> If there are any objections, they should be treated as was the original part. Start the whole process again with Step 4.

8) <u>If there is no immediate test of the desired behavior available, have the students "future pace" to the next possible time when they will be faced with a similar situation.</u> Instruct the students to tell you what is happening. Watch the students' sensory output to determine if there is a correlation between the verbal statements of the students and the students' sensory feedback. This test is the best one that can be made until the actual event comes along.

9) **Direct the student to review with confidence, pleasure and satisfaction how each part cooperated and to thank them.**

(Simplified steps for Transforming can be found on pages 232 and 233.)

Scenario To Illustrate Transformation

Lynn indicated that since grade school, despite her best efforts to work up to her academic ability (a case of underachievement), she has been unable to do so and would like to overcome what to her has become a problem. The teacher knows Lynn's background and knows that what she says is true.

T: "Lynn, if I understand you correctly, you would like to be able to work up to your academic potential. Is this statement correct?"

S: "Yes, I'd give a great deal to get better grades so I can go to college."

T: "Alright. Let's give the part that's causing this behavior a label: a nickname, a color, a letter, a number - whatever you'd like."

S: "I think I'd like to call it Zero'!"

T: "Fine. Would you go inside yourself and ask Zero if it is willing to communicate with me? This communication may come in the form of a picture, a sensory signal like warmth, or a chill, or you may experience something like an internal voice."

(The teacher waits for the student to establish communication with Zero.)

S: "Zero says it's O.K."

(Should Zero not communicate at this point the teacher should have the student ask Zero why it will not communicate. When there is a signal other than an internal auditory one (a voice or thought that comes to the student), the teacher should again have the student ask the part to intensify the signal to be certain that it is a communication from that part.)

T: "Lynn, I'd like to have you ask Zero what it has been trying to do for you."

S: "Zero says it has been afraid that I would concentrate so much on my studies that I would miss out on the fun things of life."

T: "Zero has been trying to be of help to you even though you do not always appreciate its efforts. If you feel able to thank Zero for its efforts, please do so. I also want to thank Zero for its efforts. Remember that Zero will always be available when needed. (Pause.) Each of us has a creative part. Would you contact your creative part and ask it to come up with at least three new choices to satisfy your need?"

S: Reflects for a while, then says, "O.K. I now have five choices." (Since this step is critical, be certain the choices are good ones.)

160

T: "Good! Ask Zero if it is willing to accept these five new choices to meet its need."

S: "Zero is willing to try them."

T: "Excellent! Would you again go inside and ask if there are any other parts that have a role in creating this behavior? If there are, ask them to accept the choices."

S: "No, no other parts are involved."

T: "Lynn, ask if any other parts have an objection to these new choices."

S: "No, there are no objections."

T: "Lynn, I'd like to have you go into the future and think of the next time that you would have normally been bothered by Zero. What's happening now?"

(The teacher observes sensory feedback to determine the success of the transformation.)

S: "Wow! I'm really getting the work done and I'm really doing well!"

T: "Lynn, thank all the parts both for yourself and for me."

Learning Pattern Elicitation

Individuals organize and manage their subjective experiences through simple and complex arrangements of sensory systems. These arrangements are called "learning patterns." Each of us internally processes our subjective experience, and an automatic sequencing occurs within our sensory systems. One individual may make decisions by using this sequence: $V^I \longrightarrow A_d^I \longrightarrow K^I \longrightarrow$ Exit (visual image, auditory internal dialogue and kinesthetic internal feelings). Another individual may use a slightly varied sequence to make decisions: $A_d^I \longrightarrow V^I \longrightarrow K^I \longrightarrow$ Exit. Each sensory system (V, A or K), is considered a component of the learning pattern sequence. Together, the complete sequence comprises a learning pattern.

Learning patterns allow individuals to develop and execute a behavior. Consequently, hundreds of learning patterns are created which range from what is eaten for breakfast and how it is done, to the planning of more complicated behaviors and tasks. As an example, one possible learning pattern that could be used in learning this material would be to do the following:

1) Read each chapter.

   A time could be selected when it would be easy to concentrate on reading the book.

2) Hear the words internally.

   As the book is read, the words might be heard internally.

3) Check out one's internal feelings.

161

The reader could monitor himself to determine what his body felt about the content of his reading.

4) Do the sensory-based exercises and practice the skills.

If all the internal feelings responded positively, the reader would probably do the practice exercises and practice the skills on the colleagues with whom he has done the exercises before using the skills with his students.

This sequence would be visualized in this manner: $V^e \longrightarrow A^i_d \longrightarrow K^i \longrightarrow$ Exit (visual external, auditory internal dialogue, kinesthetic internal, with "exit" being the decision to do the practice exercises).

Most students have developed at least one school survival pattern that enables them to learn new material and to cope with school. However, it frequently happens that a successful pattern is developed for a particular situation and then is applied in other situations with much less success or even outright failure. The Peter Principle of people rising to the level of their incompetence may be understood in a new light now. Teachers have seen it at work in the world of education. Often a successful teacher becomes a principal. The thinking leading to the appointment of the principal is that the good teaching patterns exhibited by the principal when he was a teacher will automatically be good patterns for being a principal. However, unless that particular teacher is flexible and has other patterns that can successfully be used in this new situation, or has adaptable patterns, that person may turn out to be a horrible principal.

The students who are classified as slow learners (without brain damage) may simply have poor learning patterns which can be altered so that more efficient and effective learning can occur. Most learning patterns are processed unconsciously. Therefore, before learning patterns can be modified, it is necessary for the teacher to be able to identify them. Learning patterns are composed of steps or sequences. Each step is associated with, and bonded to, the previous step. It is similar to putting children's toys together or making a casserole. The simplest learning pattern that enables the student to arrive at his goal is the most preferable one.

The difference between an unsuccessful learning pattern and a successful one is determined by the following specific conditions:

1) The learning pattern must have all major sensory systems involved (V, A & K).

2) The learning pattern must have a specific outcome.

3) The learning pattern must include an orderly, sequential process, a comparison, and a decision or choice point.

4) The learning pattern should have at least three options.

5) The learning pattern should have an external check - something that provides a connection to the outside world. The choices could range from a time limit, to teaching students to ask themselves at the end of the learning pattern whether they have developed three options in their learning pattern. This last external check serves as a type of future pacing.

While it is always possible that there may be exceptions to these conditions for a successful learning pattern, most will fulfill them.

Analyzing two learning patterns will illustrate how the conditions are applied. Here are two learning patterns used by two different adults to make a decision:

1) $V^e \longrightarrow V^r \longrightarrow A_d^i \longrightarrow V^r \longrightarrow V^c \longrightarrow K^i \longrightarrow$ Exit;

2) V^e or $A^e \longrightarrow K^i / K_r^i \longrightarrow V^c / V^r \longrightarrow K^i \longrightarrow A_d^i \longrightarrow K^i \longrightarrow$ Exit.

In the first learning pattern the individual:

V^e - looks at something, an object, a report, etc.

V^r - recalls a memory dealing with a time that he made a similar decision;

A_d^i - talks to himself about it;

V^r - recalls the past image or images related to the situation;

V^c - constructs an image of himself making the decision; and

K^i - checks his internal feelings to determine if his decision feels good.

In comparing this learning pattern with the conditions necessary for a successful learning pattern, it is evident that the learning pattern has all major sensory systems involved, has a specific outcome and includes an orderly sequential process. The comparison check occurs in the $V^r \longrightarrow A_d^i \longrightarrow V^r$ segment of the learning pattern. The person has recalled his visual image, replayed a past conversation and again recalled the same visual image. He then constructed a visual image (V^c). The decision or choice point occurs when he checks his feelings (K^i). Without knowing the context of the situation and the actual decision, it is difficult to determine if the learning pattern has three options or an external check.

The second learning pattern (V^e or $A^e \longrightarrow K^i / K_r^i \longrightarrow V^c / V^r \longrightarrow K^i$

$A_d^i \longrightarrow K^i \longrightarrow$ Exit), specifically deals with a decision to purchase a particular book.

The individual:

V^e or A^e - either sees a particular book advertised and/or reads an advertisement or book review about it, or hears about the book from another person;

K^i / K_r^i - checks out his present feelings about the book against his remembered feelings about books on that subject to determine his interest level;

V^c / V^r - compares himself presently buying the book with past instances of buying a book;

K^i - compares his feelings about buying the book;

A_d^i - talks to himself about his options; he can buy the book or not buy it, or

163

he can choose not to buy it at this time and buy it at a later date, or he can ask someone else to buy it for him, or he can borrow a friend's copy, or he can read it at the library, or he could ask himself what his options are, or he could decide to make the decision by a particular time;

K^i - once again, he checks his feelings against the options and decides.

The sensory-based exercises at the end of the chapter can develop your sensory acuity to gather necessary information (predicate patterns and entry cues), for identifying simple learning patterns.

Simple learning pattern elicitation starts at the beginning of the pattern. The steps that follow will be helpful in eliciting a pattern:

1) Establish rapport.

2) Guide the student through the learning pattern you are seeking to elicit by having the student recreate the pattern as you observe.

3) Watch the student's eye movement patterns and, if necessary, ask questions to clarify the learning pattern sequence.

Scenario To Illustrate the Elicitation Process
Convinced that a student having difficulty passing spelling tests has a faulty learning pattern, the teacher decides to elicit the student's learning pattern for recalling spelling words.

T: "Johnny, I'd like to see if I can find out why you have difficulty recalling your spelling words. Would you show me how you study your spelling words?"

S: "O.K."

T: "Here are several words. Let's take the first one."

(The student looks at the first word (V^e).)

T: "Johnny, pretend that you are now going to study this word for your weekly test. Show me how you would do that."

(Johnny's eyes shift down to his left (A_d^i), indicating that he is talking to himself. He then tries to write the word correctly, but he is unable to do so (K^e).)

To verify his observations, the teacher has the student attempt to recall several more words. Johnny's response is consistent.

Johnny's learning pattern sequence is:

$$V^e \longrightarrow A_d^i \longrightarrow K^e \longrightarrow Exit.$$

His difficulty lies in the fact that his learning pattern uses an auditory component and lacks a visual recall component. (Good spellers visualize words, they do not have an auditory component.)

Now proceed to elicit learning patterns by completing the following practice acitivity.

Practice Activity G - Eliciting A Learning Pattern

Find a partner. (It may be helpful to have a third person involved to help verify eye movement patterns.) Calibrate your partner's eye movement patterns. Select one or more of the following situations. (The more practice you have, the more proficient you will be at eliciting patterns.) Figure out your partner's pattern for the situation(s) selected. Record the information.

1.   How do you decide to buy a particular item?

2.   How do you study?

3.   How do you motivate yourself to mow the lawn or to perform some other task?

4.   Remember a time when you created something. Describe the steps you took in the process.

5.   How do you select the social activities in which you participate?

By now you should feel reasonably comfortable in eliciting patterns. To gain further practice, select one or more students who perform well in a particular subject and elicit their patterns in the same manner as you did in the practice activity. Next, elicit patterns from students who do not do well and compare their pattern with the students who do perform well in the same subject matter areas. What difference(s) did you find? In some instances students only need to change one sequence of their pattern or to add a sequence, in order to perform better. Space is left for you to record the elicited patterns.

Learning Pattern Installation

The processes of eliciting and installing a learning pattern are closely allied. The installation process includes:

1) all of the steps from Building Rapport through the Decision Point Frame

2) several options:

      a.   guiding students to select a successful task and, then, eliciting that success pattern, the unsuccessful pattern, and comparing the two.

      b.   eliciting the unsuccessful pattern with the idea of altering one or more components of the pattern to make it successful.

      c.   installing a pattern that has already proven successful in accomplishing the desired outcome.

Learning patterns are installed through repetition and linking. Installing patterns through repetition means that the steps are rehearsed: students are led through the steps until they automatically use them when there is a need for that pattern. Usually linking is combined with this process. Dilts (Neuro-Linguistic Programming, Vol. I, pp 231-234), discusses a case study involving the use of repetition and linking in installing learning patterns. A young girl was having difficulty both in reading and in spelling. She continually mixed up and reversed word orders and had been diagnosed by a specialist as dyslexic. Since being able to visualize internally is a vital skill for both reading and for spelling, the teacher decided to check her capacity for creating internal images. She was able to create and describe a number of images suggested by the teacher. The next step was to determine her reading and spelling patterns. The teacher held a flash card and asked the girl to read it and then spell each word. The child's eye movement patterns went down to her left (A_d^i), switched over to her right (K^i), and switched back to her left (A_d^i). Consequently, her strategy of $A_d^i \longrightarrow K^i \longrightarrow A_d^i$ completely eliminated a visual component which is a vital segment of a successful reading and spelling pattern!

Making a game out of learning pattern installation is often necessary, particularly when working with smaller children. The girl agreed to a suggestion by the teacher that they play a flash card game that would be fun and that would not require trying to learn to read or to spell. The teacher held up a flash card and as he pointed from left to right to each letter, the child was to pronounce each letter and then sound out each word. This sequence can be illustrated $V^e \longrightarrow A_d^e$. The child was then instructed to look at the entire word, say it out loud and then to look down to her right and determine from her feelings if the sounds that she was making constituted a real word. If her feelings and words were inconsistent, she was to look again at the letters, say them in a different way, and determine how she felt about the new pronunciation and the word.

Each time she correctly pronounced and read the word, the teacher linked her success by smiling, saying "Good!" while using an approving tone and by squeezing her wrist. The teacher then showed her a flash card, put it down, directed her eyes up to her left (V^r - The girl used eye movements of a normally organized right-handed person) until she could visualize the card that he had just held up. As she visualized the letter, she was to see the letter in any color she chose. Once she could clearly see the letter, she was to read the letters out loud (not spell them) as she visualized them. If she had any difficulty, the teacher was to assist her by moving his finger from left to right. She was then to visualize the words, change the color of the words if she desired, sound out the letters, look back at the letter sequence, pronounce the word, and determine the correctness of her feelings about it by putting her eyes down to her right. As she successfully completed each step, the linking process (smile, "good" and the wrist squeeze) were used.

As the game progressed, and when the child had any difficulty, the teacher made the visualization or pronunciation appear in her mind's eye by squeezing her wrist. The child was instructed to recreate any word-image or pronunciation by simply squeezing her own wrist. The teacher reported that although the child left out a letter occasionally, not a word or letter was reversed during the entire game. The child accomplished a great deal and, more importantly, felt good about it!

Notice that the emphasis was upon the process of learning rather than upon the subject matter; the learning experience was simply a game, and any difficulty that the student had was dealt with by having her change her eye movement patterns. Her original reading pattern of $V^e \longrightarrow A^i_d \longrightarrow K^i \longrightarrow A^i_d$, and her spelling pattern of $A^i_d \longrightarrow K^i \longrightarrow A^i_d$ were both inappropriate to accomplish either goal. Two new learning patterns were installed. These patterns included a sight-reading pattern $V^e_i \longrightarrow A^e_d \longrightarrow K^i \longrightarrow V^e \longrightarrow$ Exit and a spelling pattern $V^i \longrightarrow A_d \longrightarrow K^i \longrightarrow V^i \longrightarrow$ Exit.

Grinder relates a similar, but more simplified incident (Frogs Into Princes, 1979, pp. 119-120) of a child who had difficulty spelling. Giving him a list of ten words, Grinder had the boy look at them and try to tell him what the words were, rather than having him spell them. Since the boy's visualization process was not well developed, he had difficulty following Grinder's directions. Grinder decided to combine an experience from the boy's personal history with the spelling task. He asked the boy who his favorite Star Wars character was. The boy replied that his favorite character was the Wookie. Grinder had the boy visualize the spelling words in the Wookie's mouth and print them. The boy was then able to rapidly learn his spelling words. (This is an excellent example of incorporating the boy's own model of the world in the learning experience.)

Applying Developmental Techniques To The Elementary Student

The major advice regarding the application of the formalized Transforming Technique to the elementary student is to keep it as simple as possible. Make it a fun time, similar to a game time. By being flexible enough to experiment with the technique, you will emerge with a workable Transforming Technique that will meet students' needs and ultimately, your instructional goals.

Earlier in this chapter there were some suggestions made for eliciting and installing learning patterns with elementary students. The following chapter gives some specific patterns that can be installed to help children spell, learn math more easily, and to write creatively.

Exercise #50
Single-Sentence Transforming

Purpose: To develop Single-Sentence Transformers.

'A', 'B' and 'C' recall re-occurring situations in their teaching history for which Single-Sentence Transformers would be helpful. They develop appropriate meaning and/or context transformers for those situations.

The Single-Sentence Transformers are shared and critiqued.

Exercise #51
Transforming

Purpose: To learn the Transforming Technique.

'A' selects a response that incorporates secondary gain.

'B' completes the steps prior to transforming and guides 'A' through the steps.

'C' observes.

Rotate the roles.

Collateral Exercise #50

Purpose: To apply Single-Sentence Transformers to classroom situations.

The teacher uses Single-Sentence Transformers with his students as needed.

He takes particular note of the sensory feedback and the subsequent behavior of the students after delivering the Single-Sentence Transformer.

Collateral Exercise #51

Purpose: To use the Transforming Technique with a student.

The teacher chooses a student who wishes to change his behavior. The behavior designated for change must incorporate secondary gain.

The teacher guides the student through the transforming steps.

Exercise #52
Eliciting Learning Patterns

Purpose: To learn to elicit a learning pattern.

'A' selects a pattern (preferably relating to learning) that he would like to have elicited.

'B' elicits the pattern.

'C' observes.

Rotate the roles.

Collateral Exercise #52

Purpose: To install a learning pattern in a student.

The teacher chooses a student and installs a learning pattern in that student through repetition and/or linking.

Summary

Much of the emphasis in today's education dwells on presenting information, rather than on teaching learners how to learn subject matter. Learning information to become a well-rounded person and being able to apply this information in our everyday lives is the hallmark of a liberal education. If teachers were able to teach children <u>how</u> to learn by using the learning pattern elicitation and installation procedures, the goal of students becoming well-educated would become a reality.

Learning patterns, the sequencing of sensory systems to deal with an individual's subjective experience, are generally processed unconsciously. Successful patterns have all sensory systems involved, have specific outcomes, include an orderly sequential process, have a comparison and a decision point, have at least three options, and have an external check which serves as a connection to the outside world.

Learning patterns are elicited by asking questions and by watching students' eye movement patterns. Teachers should start the elicitation process at the end of the pattern and work toward its beginning. The installation of patterns most often occurs through a combination of repetition and linking. Until professionals develop more universal patterns that provide simple and effective ways to teach specific learning objectives, teachers may need to elicit learning patterns from successful students. Teachers would be making important contributions by teaching students patterns that help them master subject matter more easily.

Chapter 18

SPECIFIC LEARNING PATTERNS

It was the end of the school day and the Master was in a reflective mood. He looked back over the day remembering the satisfaction he had felt when he installed a new learning pattern in a student having difficulty with a subject. How pleased the student had been to be able to correctly complete his work in a short period of time! The Master allowed his mind to drift back to his early teaching days when he had neither the knowledge nor the skills that he now possessed. He remembered how emotionally drained and frustrated he felt because he had worked so hard trying to help his students learn, and his results had been marginally successful at best. As he looked ahead in time, he felt a rush of anticipation and interest as he thought of the many students who would benefit from his experience.

What are some specific learning patterns for math, spelling and creative writing?

Several specific learning patterns are presented in this chapter. They are excellent ones for what they seek to accomplish. In time, other patterns may be available in other subject matter areas. In the interim, teachers with exceptional students might wish to elicit patterns from those students and install them in students lacking such patterns.

Recalling Math Equations

This particular learning pattern can be used with adults as well as with younger students. The pattern is diagrammed in this manner:

$$V^e \longrightarrow V^r \longrightarrow K^e \longrightarrow V^r \longrightarrow K^e \longrightarrow V^e \longrightarrow V^r \longrightarrow K^e \longrightarrow V^e \longrightarrow V^r \longrightarrow K^e \longrightarrow \text{Exit.}$$

1) Have the student select a favorite color.

2) Ve The student looks at a math equation that is written down. (Example: $2 + 2 = 4$)

3) V^r The student shifts his eyes to his V^r position, sees the equation in his favorite color and recalls the equation.

4) K^e The student writes down the visualization.

5) V^r The student shifts his eyes V^r and recalls the equation backwards in his favorite color:

$$2 + 2 = 4$$

(The purpose of recalling the equation backward is to encourage students to visualize the equation. If this step proves unsatisfactory, eliminate it.)

6) K^e The student writes the equation backward.

7) V^e A list containing the equation plus several similar equations is presented.

8) V^r The student places his eyes in his V^r position and recalls the equation in his favorite color.

9) K^e The student writes down the correct equation.

10) Ve Another list containing the equation plus several similar equations is presented for completion.

     Example: $2 + 2 = $ _____

                             $4 + 1 = $ _____

                             $3 + 3 = $ _____

11) V^r The student places his eyes in his V^r position and recalls the correct equation in his favorite color.

12) K^e The student writes the correct equation and its answer on a sheet of paper.

Recalling Spelling Words

The spelling pattern is the same as the math pattern, but has some variations. The best spellers visualize words, they do not sound them out. Therefore, there is no auditory component in this pattern, and there is no component for visualizing the word backwards. The pattern is symbolized in the same manner:

$$V^e \longrightarrow V^r \longrightarrow K^e \longrightarrow V^r \longrightarrow K^e \longrightarrow V^e \longrightarrow V^r \longrightarrow K^e \longrightarrow V^e \longrightarrow V^r \longrightarrow K^e \longrightarrow Exit.$$

1) Have the student select a favorite color.

2) Ve The student visualizes the total word or part of the word. (It may be easier for the beginning student to chunk down and visualize the spelling of only three letters of a word at a time. For example, "b e l i e v e." Steps 2 through 4 are repeated until the entire word is learned.)

3) V^r The student shifts his eyes into his V^r position and sees or recalls that part of the word that he is learning, or the entire word.

4) K^e The student copies down the word.

5) V^r The student again shifts his eyes in his V^r position and, in his favorite color, visualizes the word. He copies it down backwards.

b e l i e v e

(The purpose of recalling the word backward is to encourage students to visualize the word. If this step proves unsatisfactory, eliminate it.)

6) K^e The student writes down the word backwards.

7) Ve The student examines a list of words.

Example: a) bilieve

b) believe

c) beleive

d) bealeave

e) beleev

f) beleave

8) V^r The student shifts his eyes in his V^r position and recognizes the correct spelling of the word from the list.

9) K^e The student writes down the correct word.

10) Ve The student examines a sentence containing the spelling word.

Example: "How do you spell believe?"

11) V^r The student shifts his eyes to his V^r position and recalls the color-coded word.

12) K^e The student corrects the spelling word if it is incorrectly spelled, or he writes a "C" next to the sentence if the word is spelled correctly.

These recall skills improve by practice rather than by rereading the math problem or spelling words. As the student's recall ability improves, he will be able to have more accurate recall under the stress of an exam.

A Learning Pattern For Writing Creatively

Writing creatively can be a fun and reasonably simple process when this learning pattern is employed:

$$V^c \longrightarrow A^c \longrightarrow K^i \longrightarrow A^i_d \longrightarrow K^e \longrightarrow \text{Exit.}$$

1) V^c The student places his eyes in his V^c context and thinks about what responses he would like to have from his reader(s). Then he determines what images would get that response.

2) A^c The student shifts his eyes to his A^c position and listens for any sounds or noises connected with the response that he wishes his reader(s) to have. He examines the different aspects of the experience in an effort to hear some meaningful sounds and noises that can generate the desired response.

3) K^i The student shifts his eyes in his K position to sift through the various feelings associated with the experience, so that he can select the most powerful ones to elicit the responses that he seeks from his reader(s).

172

4) A_d^i The student places his eyes in his A_d^i position and talks to himself about what words can best get his desired reader response(s). He can ask himself what different people and/or characters would say about his topic. He can ask himself if his examination of what to say about the topic gives him any ideas of other ways to talk about his topic.

5) K^e The student writes his topic.

Motivation Patterns

By having material presented in the major sensory systems (V, A & K), students will be motivated automatically by the images, sounds and feelings that such teaching engenders. Also, by reversing students' main learning patterns, motivation occurs automatically. If their pattern is V⟶A⟶K⟶Exit, then the pattern could be reversed by asking the students how it would feel (K), to listen (A) to and watch (V) a film on a particular subject. This reversing of the pattern has the effect of bringing students to the beginning of their learning pattern, so that they will be highly motivated to complete the assignment or task. Students can also have their own motivation patterns in non-academic areas elicited and applied to academic areas. For example, student-athletes who excel in a sport and who are highly motivated to play that sport, but who are not motivated to excel in class can have their sports motivation pattern elicited and installed so that academically, they will be more highly motivated. Like the earlier patterns discussed in this chapter, installation of the motivation pattern would be accomplished through repetition and through linking.

Exercise #53
Installing A Learning Pattern

Purpose: To learn to install a learning pattern in a friend, family member or colleague.

'A' selects a learning pattern that he would like to integrate.

'B' installs the learning pattern.

'C' observes.

Rotate the roles.

Collateral Exercise #53

Purpose: To learn to install a learning pattern in a student.

The teacher selects a student who could benefit from the installation of an entire learning pattern or of a component of a learning pattern. (The learning pattern can be elicited by the teacher or someone else.)

The teacher can elicit the pattern if he wishes to examine the components of the pattern, or simply install one. He tests the pattern after it is installed.

Summary

This chapter has suggested specific learning patterns for math, spelling, and for creative writing. Students' motivation patterns and ways to install them have been discussed. Remember that repetition and/or linking will aid installation of learning patterns and will enable students to more rapidly work on their own. You are encouraged to elicit patterns and to install them as they are needed. Eliciting and installing learning patterns can be a very rewarding and interesting experience!

Notes

Chapter 19

ADDITIONAL LEARNING PATTERNS

Jeff Stokes had been an excellent student throughout elementary school. Although he was extremely conscientious and spent hours every night doing homework, each year of junior high school had been more difficult. His grades were now down to "C's" and "D's". His initial evaluation showed only two problem areas. First, because Jeff was anxious about his performance, he spent much of the time accessing his feelings and talking to himself. Secondly, he wasn't making pictures when he read. Jeff spent a total of eight sessions with a New Learning Pathways^{TM} consultant. In just a few sessions, he learned about the importance of making pictures as he read. Jeff was absolutely amazed at the immediate effect making pictures had on his ability to comprehend. He stopped being tense about not understanding the material and studying even became interesting to him. By the end of the quarter, Jeff's grades were up to C's and B's. Last summer, Jeff reported that the past year had been his easiest ever, and that his last report card was covered with A's and B's.

Darcy had been receiving special remedial help for two years after a full battery of tests indicated both visual and auditory perceptual difficulties. Although she had been drilled again and again, she just couldn't seem to grasp phonics. Her total reading score was more than two years below grade level. Darcy had frequent stomach aches before school and said she hated reading. Her initial evaluation revealed that she did little internal visual processing for learning tasks. It also seemed Darcy was having visual focus problems too. To check this out, the consultant moved back six feet from her and used flashcards with large print. Within ten minutes, Darcy easily and joyfully learned eight difficult reading words. She was even able to spell five of them. (Her spelling list consisted of three and four-letter words.) With the application of strategies, such as those described in this chapter and vision therapy, learning began to be exciting for Darcy. Her stomach aches disappeared and her test scores jumped one and a half years in the first eight-week increment. Now, a year later, Darcy is near the top of her class and reading is one of her favorite subjects.

What are the additional learning patterns? What are the steps involved in the patterns?

New Learning Pathways^{TM}, a Colorado and California based NLP educational consulting company, has as its motto "We don't believe in 'learning disabilities'". In the five years this company has been in existence its founders, Mary Jane Brownell and June Jackson, have had great success developing and applying NLP learning patterns, or strategies, to students who have been diagnosed as having "learning disabilities." They have found that many students who are classified as having "learning disabilities," actually have poor learning patterns, or visual problems of the type which are frequently not diagnosed in a general eye examination. They have been able to assist those students who have poor learning patterns by determining the missing components in the learning patterns of those students and to change the patterns so that the students may learn more easily.

Whenever possible, New Learning Pathways[TM] works on an incremental basis wi.. a defined number of sessions. In most instances, a specific goal is guaranteed. Should the student not make the expected growth in learning, additional sessions would be given at no charge or the clients money would be returned[7]. For example, New Learning Pathways[TM] guarantees one year's growth in phonetic analysis, comprehension, retention and work comprehension, (analogies), in eight hourly sessions that are spread out over an eight-week period. This guarantee is based on a pre and post test measurement using the Woodcock Reading Mastery and the Ekwall Reading Inventory.

The parents have an important role in the guarantee. Toward the end of each learning session, a parent is trained to reinforce the child's newly-learned pattern. Throughout the period of time that New Learning Pathways[TM] is working with the student, the patterns are being reinforced at home for 15 to 20 minutes per day. (If either parent is unable to work with their child because of lack of time, or patience, another person can be trained to work with the child. This could be a neighbor, an older teenager or grandparent. The person selected <u>must</u> have rapport with the student, a loving sense of humor, and a strong belief that the student <u>can</u> learn.) As long as the patterns are being reinforced consistently during the eight weeks, the New Learning Pathways[TM] guarantee is valid.

After the initial goals have been met through weekly sessions, monthly "brush-up" sessions are held for three to six months. These sessions aid the student in integrating the necessary skills into his classroom. As soon as the student and his parents are satisfied with the integration, the monthly structured program allows the student and his parents to make the necessary adjustments so that the new learning pattern can be positively transferred to the classroom.

The publishing of the New Learning Pathways[TM] learning patterns in this book marks the first time that these learning patterns have been published.

The Initial Evaluation

Before working with any student, an initial evaluation is held. The New Learning Pathway[TM] goals for the evaluation are to:

1)   establish rapport.

2)   gather information about the student's favored thinking channel, (dominant sensory system), in order to be able to initially pace the student.

      This is done by observing posture, listening for predicates, etc.

---

[7]Two types of cases are not always guaranteed: 1) a student with a severe visual problem, (see more about vision therapy later in this chapter); 2) a "passive" student that uses his academics as a "power play" with his family. Short term family counseling may be suggested to deal with the learning issues involved in working with the "passive" student.

3)   check for congruence between the student's learning goals and the parent's goals for the student.

Both parents and students are asked what they will see and hear. For example, the parents may say, "We just want him to have a better attitude about school." The response is, "What will you see and hear that will indicate that your son or daughter has a better attitude about school?" A student may say, "I want Mom and Dad off my back." The response is, "What do you want them to do? What will you see and hear if they are being supportive and are not bugging you?"

4)   access basic strategies or patterns for math, reading, following instructions, and spelling.

This is accomplished by having the student do tasks like: reading a short passage to determine his comprehension strategy; following instructions; spelling words; doing math facts and completing a couple of math problems. Watching a student's physiology will give information about his learning patterns. For example, watching a student's eye movements as he spells will tell whether he is using a visual or an auditory spelling pattern. (Patterns can be accessed as described in Chapter 18.)

5)   screen for basic visual skills for learning.

If there are any questions about the student's visual abilities, the student is referred for vision testing. (See the next section for more information about vision testing.)

Vision Problems and Vision Therapy

An estimated 75 to 90 percent of all classroom learning occurs through visual channels. Any interference with these channels can cause difficulty with learning tasks. Most children are born with healthy eyes and structures. However, vision is a learned process, and is something more than 20/20 visual acuity. Vision enables individuals to gather, analyze, process, store and respond to light information. Children may see 20/20, but still suffer from severe visual difficulties. Therefore, it is essential that vision, our dominant sense, be adequately developed and enhanced to prevent vision problems.

What are the visual skills necessary for school achievement?

1)   Eye movement skills (pursuits, fixations)

2)   Eye teaming skills (eye alignment, focus)

3)   Eye hand coordination skills

4)   Visual form perception (visual comparison, visual imagery, visualization).

What are the symptoms a teacher could observe if a student has problems with these skills?

1)   One eye turns in or out at any time.

2)	Headaches occur especially after reading or when they are performing sustained near work.

3)	Blurring, double vision, and/or eye discomfort occurs.

4)	The student frequently loses his place during reading.

5)	The student needs to use a finger or marker when reading.

6)	The student omits small words and/or letters.

7)	The student rereads lines.

8)	One eye is covered, or the student squints or closes his eye or eyes.

9)	The head is tilted.

10)	The book is held too closely to the student's face, or the student's face is too close to the reading material on the desk.

11)	The student writes crookedly, spaces his work poorly, and cannot stay on ruled lines.

12)	Students beyond the age of seven are confused about left-right directions.

13)	Likenesses and differences are confused.

14)	The student fails to recognize the same word in the next sentence.

15)	As the student continues to read, comprehension is reduced.

16)	The student makes errors copying material.

17)	The student experiences difficulty in catching or hitting balls.

18)	The student has poor coordination.

Most students do not necessarily exhibit all of these symptoms. However, if a student shows several of these symptons, he should be examined to check whether glasses, contact lenses, or vision therapy may be necessary.

Vision therapy is the art and science of developing visual abilities to achieve optimal visual performance. The therapy helps prevent the development of some vision problems, aids in proper development of visual abilities, enhances the efficiency and comfort of visual functioning, and helps remediate existing vision problems. Vision therapy is a specialty of vision care found in behavioral or developmental optometric practices.[9]

---

[9]To find a doctor specializing in functional vision care, contact your state Optometric Association or write: College of Optometrists in Vision Department, P.O. Box 285, Chula Vista, CA 92012, or The Optometric Extension Program, 2912 S. Daimler, Santa Ana, CA 92705. (Dr. Lynn Fishman Hellerstein, an optometrist located in Englewood, CO, assisted in the development of the NLP strategies in this chapter.)

Parents making an appointment with an eye doctor should ask the following questions:

1) Do you give a full series of near point visual tests?

2) Do you give academically related visual perception tests?

3) Do you provide vision therapy in your office? If not, do you refer to a doctor who does give vision therapy?

4) Will you send a written report that may be used to understand and assist the child?

5) Will you see this child again during the school year to ascertain his progress?

Students with vision problems are frequently mislabelled or misunderstood. Many students labelled "learning disabled," "dyslexic," "behavior problems," "slow," etc., have undiagnosed visual problems. Vision may not be the only deficient area, but it definitely needs to be evaluated. Yearly vision examinations are recommended for children after the age of three. Adults are encouraged to have visual examinations every two years.

Behavioral Change Steps

Most educators would agree that when an individual learns to think differently, he has to go through a number of steps to internalize this new way of thinking. New Learning Pathways^{TM} presupposes that individuals who learn new behavioral patterns go through specific steps before that change comes about. (Some teachers need to be reminded that this process of internalizing a new way of thinking differs from the pattern that a student uses in storing rote information.) The process of making the change can be made more enjoyable if the person making the change gives credit to himself for his progress, or is given credit for his progress at every step.

1) Step One involves gathering new information, reading books, attending workshops, talking to people, etc. <u>Somehow the individual decides to change.</u>

2) In Step Two, the individual behaves in the old manner and realizes <u>after</u> he behaves in the old manner, that he has done it the old, (or undesirable), way.

   (This is time for congratulations! The individual is past Step One.)

3) In Step Three, the individual realizes <u>while he is in the process,</u> that he is behaving the old way and that he wants to do it differently.

   (Again, congratulations! The individual is moving right along now.)

4) In Step Four, the individual makes a conscious decision <u>as he proceeds</u> to behave differently. While the results are better and better, the individual may still be aware of some awkwardness.

5) In Step Five, the new behavior is automatic, and the individual notices that he has done just what he has wanted to do. At this stage, the new behavior

is integrated into other personal resources. The individual can then use his creativity to express the new behavior in his own unique way.

(Congratulations on a job well done! Remember to celebrate the new accomplishment.)

A Pattern Which Causes Learning Disabilities

When a student who has experienced failure in the past is presented with a new task, old painful experiences may be triggered, causing stress. Negative pictures and sounds from the past take the student down into negative K, and in negative self-talk, (A_d^i). This pattern prevents the student from processing external information appropriately. Consequently, any testing that is done when a student is using this pattern will not indicate the student's real level of ability.

The Following Instructions Pattern

Many students who have difficulty following verbal and written instructions may test to have auditory or visual sequencing problems. Frequently, the students can be observed in internal dialogue and internal K. Students who find it easy to follow instructions create a visual image of themselves doing the task. This enables them to "see" if more information is required before they begin. Immediate mental feedback creates a trial run which eliminates mistakes <u>before</u> they are made. Therefore, moving the student into a visual state where he <u>sees himself</u> following instructions, automatically takes him into a resourceful physiology, and away from the negative K.

When teaching this pattern, the teacher should give instructions for a task which they are certain the student can perform. (Written instructions must be able to be read by the student, and verbal instructions must be given at an appropriate vocabulary level.)

The teacher first gives simple, one-step instructions. While he is talking, the student is looking up and seeing himself (V^c). When the student has mastered those simple instructions and then carries out the task, the teacher gives instructions for more complex sequential tasks. Within a short period of time, these movements will become automatic. In the beginning it is helpful to include a number of playful or humorous instruction among the more serious ones. (For example, "Count to five. Clap your hands. Sit down and make a noise like a frog.") This technique will help to hold the child's attention.

Verbal Instructions

1)   Give instructions to the student.

2)   Direct the student to look up and to his right and see himself carrying out the instructions. (This action assumes that the student's V^c position is normal.)

3)   The student proceeds to carry out the instructions.

Written Instructions

1)   The student begins by reading simple one-step instructions and then proceeds directly to Step 2.

2)   The student looks up to his right and sees himself doing whatever was written. (Again, this assumes that the student's V^c position is normal.)

3)   He then proceeds to carry out the instructions.

If any questions arise as the student sees himself carrying out the instructions, he should get clarification and then repeat the process. As the student gains confidence, additional instructions are given. Soon, the student can picture himself doing two, three, or more tasks sequentially in a successful way.

The Reading Comprehension Pattern

New Learning Pathways^{TM} has had great success using the following reading pattern or strategy. It is not unusual for students to increase their reading level two or three years as a result of learning new patterns.

Every reading teacher has probably had students who have struggled through phonics, and can "read the words," but have not comprehended what they have read. Retention can be so poor that one sentence later students cannot remember what they have read. By observing their eye movements in response to comprehension questions, (A^r to A^c), teachers will observe these students attempting to retrieve the rote sound of words. Students will try to store an auditory sequence of the words without transferring the words into pictures in their minds. The student frequently states, "I don't remember what it said."

Students who have done little visualization in the past tend to make pictures which are very sparse in detail and poor in quality. They may leave out one of the senses, i.e. they may not even hear sounds at all. They may even leave out submodalities, the major components of our senses. A partial list of submodalities follows.

Visual	Auditory	Kinesthetic	O/G
shapes	volume	texture	taste
color	pitch	temperatures	smell
black/white	pace	movement-speed	
movement	number of sounds	emotions	
size	location	pressure	
perspective	rhythm	location	

When the student leaves out a sensory system. or major submodalities within a sensory system, the teacher can help him make better pictures by asking questions that incorporate many submodalities. Using a higher voice with a more rapid tempo will unconsciously stimulate the student to process visually. (Chapter 21 deals with submodalities in greater detail.)

An effective comprehension pattern requires that external words stimulate constructed images (V^c), and be stored in many areas in the brain. The more senses that are involved in understanding, the more "sense" the reading material will make. The goal of the New Learning Pathways^{TM} reading comprehension pattern is to establish a neural

182

pathway so that the word-to-picture process becomes automatic. This pattern is so effective that dramatic changes occur very rapidly.

Reading Comprehension Steps

1) The teacher selects reading material of real interest, <u>above</u> instructional level, to read <u>to</u> the student.

   The student's physiology should stimulate his visual processing. The student should sit upright and look in his V^c position as he watches a "movie" in his mind while the teacher reads.

2) After a couple of sentences, the teacher stops and asks specific questions about the pictures the student has made. Once the responses are appropriate and accurate, the number of sentences read before questioning can be increased.

3) After the above exercise is completed, the student can be "tested" to show him that he really does know how to make great pictures and the answers are <u>in</u> the pictures that he has made.

   This "testing" takes the form of questions about what the teacher read to the student. Most students will access their V^r to answer the questions. (Others may defocus and stare ahead.)

4) If the responses tend to still be inaccurate, too much material at one time has been covered. The teacher should go back and stop more frequently to question before going on. This process will build up the student's ability to visualize and to comprehend, and it will build his confidence.

5) Once the student has excellent ability to comprehend as the teacher reads, the student is ready to follow the same process as he reads out loud.

   Now the teacher should select material a bit lower than instructional level. The object at this point is to establish comprehension which emphasizes the student's ability to visualize and which demphasizes reliance upon an auditory strategy.

6) The teacher begins sentence by sentence, then proceeds to two sentences, etc., moving to a larger amount of material between the questioning. The student looks up to his V^c to see what he has read. When the student is "tested", he uses his V^r to remember what he has read.

7) Homework: the teacher has the student find a supportive person, (not necessarily the parents), to spend 15 minutes every evening continuing this process.

8) The same process is repeated as the student reads silently.

The typical ineffectual reading pattern leaves out V^c with submodalities (sm). The desired reading strategy would look like this: $V_e \longrightarrow A_d^i \longrightarrow V_{sm}^c$. Later, speed reading would delete the A_d^i.

Contextual Analysis

In addition to a comprehension problem, these students almost always have poor contextual analysis skills. They will read past a totally anomalous word which doesn't belong and fail to notice that it doesn't fit. Once a student has a rich, detailed internal picture which includes color, sound, and movement, (V,A,K), he will no longer be able to read past words that obviously do not make sense, because the word will seem strange in the picture that he has made. For example, a sentence reads: "The children did the math problems upon the skateboard." From his prior pictures in a classroom, the student will realize immediately that the word should be "blackboard," instead or "skateboard," and will self-edit the word. (Frequently, the student's non-verbal response will be to pull back abruptly when he says the inappropriate word.) This is the essence of contextual analysis.

Dealing With Visual Focus Problems

If it is suspected that a student has a visual focus problem, the following suggestions will be helpful. (These suggestions are not meant to replace appropriate treatment, but will make it possible for these students to experience success while they are getting or are waiting to receive treatment.)

1) Use a central focus position for both V^r and V^c. This position would have the student looking straight ahead, or slightly upward. It is not appropriate for extended work because students with visual focus problems frequently experience discomfort when trying to keep their eyes in the peripheral positions.

2) Move back four to six feet away from the student to present new words or phonetic patterns. Use a large magic marker to make flashcards that have words printed on them that are 3/4 to 1 inch large. Enlarging book pages will also help.

3) Tilt books vertically or have the student rest the book upright on a stack of books on the desk. The goal is to have the student gaze straight ahead instead of downward as he reads. (There is an inexpensive plexiglass cookbook holder on the market which will perform this function very well.)

4) Have the student use a paper marker as he reads.

5) Write paragraphs or stories on a flipchart in large print. The student can take them home and put them up in his room.

The Spelling Pattern

The New Learning Pathways^{TM} spelling pattern incorporates many NLP techniques. It is designed for application to individual students, but it can be adapted to a regular classroom setting. Teachers may wish to try both spelling patterns described in this book to see which best meets their needs.

The steps are as follows:

1) Build Rapport

The teacher should use his own strategies for putting the student at ease and then add the NLP techniques of "pacing" and "leading" that are described in

Chapter 9. If rapport is lost at any time, the teaching process should be stopped immediately, and rapport regained.

2) <u>Calibrate</u>

Determine the student's V^r position by asking questions that require visual recall. If there is any question about where the student best remembers pictures, then the teacher should periodically observe the student and make the determination.

3) <u>Linking</u>

Have the student find a successful time in his experience when he felt <u>very</u> positive about himself. (For example, learning to ride a bike, scoring a soccer goal, winning a ribbon in a Science Fair, etc...)
When the non-verbal feedback indicates the child is accessing the experience, link or anchor it by using a specific touch, gesture, or rate of speech.

If necessary, link any other positive and resourceful experiences in the same manner. As the student succeeds, the positive link should be activated. This action will reinforce and strengthen it.

It is also helpful to separate the student's "old way" of spelling by using a different touch, gesture, tonality, or slower rate of speech.

4) <u>Installing the V/K Pattern</u>

<u>Encoding the word</u>: To assure initial success, the first unknown words selected should be easy, interesting, and with good structure. The words should be written on a large flashcard with a felt tip marker; the card should be held up in the student's V^r field. The student should trace the letters with his eyes, noting the shape of the word, and the letters above and below the line. He should note in particular any double letters and the first and last letters of the word.

At this point, stop and ask some questions about the student's internal picture. Is he able to see more clearly with his eyes open or closed? If he is having difficulty making a picture, ask him to "Remember what the word looked like.", or "Just imagine what the word looked like." Another option is to have the student put the word on a TV screen. (Never give the student an option of not seeing the picture by asking if he can see it.) If necessary, improve the picture by using some of the submodalities listed in this chapter or in Chapter 21.

Remove the card and ask the student, "Is your picture clear enough? As soon as it's clear, write the word down."

<u>Utilization</u>: All responses should be utilized to get the desired outcome of visually representing the spelling word. The old "auditory" pattern for spelling can be validated by telling the student to be sure and keep the old pattern for times that he needs to spell a word that he's never seen before. The V-K strategy will show the best results for spelling.

In teaching the strategy, use any "mistakes" the student makes to get a

185

clearer picture of the word or feeling about whether it looks right. If a student reverts to the old "auditory" pattern while trying to store the word in memory, say "When you hear yourself saying the word, let that remind you to make a clearer picture."

5)   <u>Review</u>: Have the student look at each flashcard briefly in front of him and then compare it with his visually remembered image of the word to make sure they are the same.

If at this point, there is any doubt that the student has encoded the word, reintroduce the card one more time. (It also may be necessary in some cases to "chunk down" the word.)

The student should write the word. He should of course rely on his visual recall of the word as needed.

<u>Kinesthetic Check</u>: The student should compare the completed word against the picture to determine if it is spelled correctly. Say to the student, "See if that feels right."

Some students may not have an internal sense of the word "looking right or wrong". One way to develop this kinesthetic check is to notice the body feedback when the student spells the word incorrectly. Have the student pay attention to that feedback from his body. Some students will jerk back, grimace or tilt their head when the word they've written doesn't match their internal picture.

When the word "looks right" and "feels right", link the correct response and give the student one more look at the flashcard. If his answer is incorrect, return the flashcard to the area where his V^r is located, and repeat the procedure.

The Problem-Solving Pattern

The Problem-Solving Pattern can be used by teachers, in brief counseling situations, to help students. This pattern combines left and right brain activity to bring about an awareness of <u>patterns</u>, (extremely important as a base for logic), and <u>possibilities</u>. The more choices an individual has in any given situation, the more likely one is to get precisely the result he wants! These steps should be followed:

1)   <u>Outcome Statement</u>: Help the student determine a positive outcome.

2)   <u>Results Wanted</u>: Ask the student, "When you have the solution, what kinds of things will you see?" (His eyes should move to his V^c position.)

Then ask, "When you have the solution, what kinds of things will you hear?" (His eyes should move to his A^c position.)

Ask the final question, "When you have the solution, what kinds of things will you feel?" (His eyes should move to his K position.)

3)   <u>Past Actions...Future Outcomes</u>: Ask the student, "How could you make <u>absolutely certain</u> the same problem occurred again?" (His eyes should move to his V^r and then his V^c positions.) This question should result in <u>humor</u>, <u>curiosity, and resourcefulness</u>. Nobody ever has a student <u>try</u> to make a

problem occur. Obviously, students, (like all individuals), are <u>competent</u> at creating their own problems.

As the pattern proceeds, the components of the cause of the problem will be evident <u>and</u> the student will have to take responsibility for his part in creating it. This is a powerful, yet gentle move away from being a "victim" and feeling helpless.

4)   <u>Process</u>: Say to the student, "Now, let's pretend that you are <u>watching yourself</u> in a movie and see what other things you <u>might</u> do in this situation." (The student's eyes should move to his V^c position.)

It may be necessary to remind the student that in a movie the lines can be changed, different actors or actresses can appear, new "props" can be utilized, costumes can be changed, the set, lighting, etc. can also be changed, and scenes can be added or deleted.

If the first choices are even worse than the problem, all the better! The possible results will be correspondingly worse and the student <u>can see</u> that immediately. This is a good opportunity for playfulness, exaggeration, etc. When the practical ideas emerge, it will be time to move on to the next step.

5)   <u>Decision</u>: Say to the student, "Now select the best choice or choices and imagine you are actually taking action."

"What do you <u>see</u> now?" (His eyes should go to his V^c position.)

"What are you <u>saying</u> to yourself?" (His eyes should go to his A_d^i position.)

"What do you hear around you?" (His eyes should go to his A^c position.)

"How do you feel?" (His eyes should go to his K position.)

This is a reality-based check and will often make the student aware of slight changes that would be important to make in the new action before proceeding; if any changes need to be incorporated, simply repeat Step 5 with the new variation(s).

Should none of the ideas be appropriate, return to Step 4 and proceed through the steps.

Exercise #54
Installing A Learning Pattern

Purpose: To learn to install a learning pattern in a friend, family member or colleague.

'A' selects a learning pattern that he would like to integrate.

'B' installs the learning pattern.

'C' coaches and observes.

Rotate the roles.

Collateral Exercise #54

Purpose: To learn to install one of the learning patterns in this chapter.

The teacher selects a student who could benefit from the installation of one of the learning patterns in this chapter, and installs the pattern.

Summary

The New Learning Pathways[TM] learning patterns are well-developed, proven patterns that have had successful results with many students. Teachers are encouraged to try the patterns with their students, and if necessary to modify them to fit their particular situations. Teachers should be ready for some rapid positive changes! (For information on New Learning Pathway's[TM] teacher training, see the section entitled "NLP Training".)

Chapter 20

METAPHORS

One dark evening as a farmer passed a well, he heard a cry for help from its depths. "What is happening?", he yelled down. A voice replied, "I am a teacher, and I have accidentally fallen into this well. I am unable to free myself." "Keep cool and I'll fetch a rope or ladder," responded the farmer. "Just a moment please!", said the teacher. "Your grammar and diction need to be improved; kindly make the necessary changes!" "If that is what seems most important to you," angrily stated the farmer, "then I suggest you stay where you are until I learn to speak correctly!" And he proceeded on his way.

What are "Metaphors?" What are their uses? How can they be constructed?

Throughout history, anecdotes, parables and stories have been used to guide and to influence people. These anecdotes, parables and stories are also called metaphors. Metaphors may be used to illustrate a point, to command a student to do something or to avoid something, and to handle student resistance.[10]

Metaphors may seem vague or irrelevant with no meaning on a conscious basis, but when metaphors are properly constructed and presented, each students' unconscious, like a computer will scan automatically through his experiences and models to make sense out of this new experience. Students consciously, or more often unconsciously, process what they hear and apply the information to their particular situation. Consequently, metaphors can serve as profound agents of change.

People generally attempt change in two ways: by talking to others and convincing them it would be to their advantage to change, and by creating experiences that involve others. Experiences create the most change in people. Metaphors provide vicarious internal experiences for students. These experiences are non-threatening and, with the exception of the metaphor teller's imagination and ability, metaphor analogies are limitless.

The basic steps involved in constructing a metaphor are:

1) Identify The Problem Situation

The teacher identifies what happens to the students that keeps them from achieving an outcome. Of particular importance are the students internal and external behaviors. (Internal behaviors would be a component of a learning pattern - such as students making a picture and saying something to themselves $V^i \longrightarrow A_d^i$.)

___

[10]Technically, metaphors are developmental in nature and are part of the Developmental Frame. They have been placed in a separate chapter for organizational reasons and to underscore their importance.

2) Gathering The Necessary Information

(Use the following questions to make certain that pertinent information is obtained):

a.   What people are involved?

b.   What events are involved?

c.   What changes do you think students should make?

d.   What changes do the students want to make? (Sometimes students do not know what they should do. Also, the changes must be within the students' control.)

e.   How have students coped with the situation in the past or what is it that prevents students from effectively dealing with the situation?

3) Building The Metaphor

a.   Develop The Context

When metaphors are developed, certain presuppositions are made. These presuppositions may take the form of assumptions that the teacher makes in his analogy. Such assumptions may include the teacher's belief that he has identified the student's problem and that he knows the information necessary to change the student's perspective to help resolve his problem. Furthermore, each metaphor has built-in constraints which will influence the student. A final consideration is that presuppositions must be part of each student's experiences.

The metaphor should be identifiable. Students need to be able to relate to the story.

The metaphor should be compelling. It should reorient students' thinking, if just for a moment. Compelling metaphors can create expectation, or puzzlement, or desire, or excitement.

The metaphor analogy will never be an exact match. It should establish some similarities between its context and the problem context of students. The analogy should be sequential. That is, it should move step by step towards its objective rather than taking a quantum leap directly to its objective.

b.   Construct The Metaphor

Metaphor construction should include all the information that has been discussed up to this point. The metaphor outcome can either lead to a desired end or it can be open-ended, with the students deciding what the end result should be.

Metaphors are designed for change at a later time. Their immediate impact is important but change will not generally occur at that time. Because students have similar behavior patterns that operate in other contexts, the metaphor may also create behavioral changes in

191

those contexts.

4) Telling The Metaphor

The metaphor is best told in person, as opposed to writing it or telling it over the telephone, because the teacher needs to take into account students' sensory feedback and other responses and can then make any needed adjustments. Pacing students is an essential part of telling metaphors.

Like any other skill, metaphor construction and telling takes practice. The results, however, are well worth the effort needed to become proficient at this process!

Exercise #55
Analyzing Metaphor Construction

Purpose: To learn metaphor construction.

'A', 'B' and 'C' select one particular metaphor that is used in this book. Each analyzes that metaphor to determine how the basic steps of metaphor building have been followed. The findings are then shared.

Exercise #56
Construction Metaphors

Purpose: To learn to construct metaphors.

Phase I

'A', 'B' and 'C' select one particular situation or experience that would be appropriate for metaphor usage. All three work together to construct one metaphor for that situation.

Phase II

'A', 'B' and 'C' select a particular situation or experience for which each would like to develop a metaphor. Each constructs an appropriate metaphor. Metaphors are shared and critiqued.

Collateral Exercises #55 and #56

Purpose: To construct and to use a metaphor in the classroom.

The teacher selects a situation that lends itself to metaphor construction and usage.

He constructs and delivers the metaphor and notes any subsequent change over a period of time.

Summary

If teachers were to use more metaphors it would open up for them and their students a vast new frontier for exploration. Metaphors are powerful agents of long-term change. When properly constructed the effects that metaphors have can be amazing. Consequently, it will be to the teacher's advantage to anticipate situations where metaphors will be useful and to construct several metaphors which can be used for those occasions. At first metaphor construction may be difficult, but once the necessary skills are honed and practiced, construction will be more enjoyable and interesting. The telling of metaphors should utilize the sensory responses of students.

Chapter 21

SUBMODALITY PATTERNS

The student found the Master reading, of all things, an agricultural journal. Puzzled, the student asked him why he would ever read a journal so far removed from his field. The Master said, "I found this article fascinating. It describes a new method of planting corn that increases production, while at the same time lowering costs. It also serves as a reminder to me that we humans frequently fall into a trap of thinking that we are very knowledgeable in our fields of specialization. Then along comes a new development, or technique, that gets results much more rapidly, and we realize how little we really know." "I would think this would be very frustrating," replied the student. "On the contrary," the Master replied, "it is a great challenge. As long as we continue to learn and to serve, we remain vital, and alive. The farmer can teach us many things. The way that we sow our seeds and tend our crops has a direct outcome on what we harvest."

Richard Bandler, the co-founder of NLP, has been characterized as "...the creative genius behind NLP." This characterization is particularly evident in his most recent work. Bandler reminds us that, in most people's lives, behavioral change is a continual, on-going process. Furthermore, this change process occurs easily and naturally, and it is generally outside our conscious awareness. Bandler's curiosity has led to a discovery of additional processes that the brain uses to bring about change. Connirae and Steve Andreas have recently become the chief organizers, systematizers, and teachers of Bandler's work. Along with Bandler, they continue to experiment with, refine the techniques, and develop new change patterns.[11]

The direction of NLP has always been to learn more about the subjective experience of learning. Much of our learning is objective, it centers around learning facts and how best to teach those facts to students. It also studies students who have learning difficulties rather than students who learn a particular subject well. How the learner learns, how he processes information has generally been ignored. If the learner has this knowledge, he will have more control over his own experience and consequently over what is learned. As we have seen in Chapter 17, students have learning patterns or strategies that they use to learn, or attempt to learn, subject matter. If the teacher has already elicited a good learning pattern for a particular subject, he can elicit the pattern of a student having difficulty learning, and he can then change the pattern so that learning occurs more easily.

This chapter further refines the work done in Chapters 17, 18, and 19, and suggests new techniques that can lead to increased learning.

What are "Submodalities" and "Submodality Patterns" How can they be utilized?

---

[11] The information in this chapter is drawn from the work of Bandler and the Andreases. The Andreases offer various high quality national NLP workshops. Their publishing house, Real People Press publishes several excellent titles. (See Bibliography for a partial listing.)

Submodalities

"Modalities" is an NLP term used to describe the components of our "sensory systems". We process information through the various modalities of our sensory system: visual, auditory, and kinesthetic. Submodalities are smaller components within each modality, or individual sensory unit. The following are examples of submodalities.[12]

Visual Submodalities

Brightness	Color	Clarity
Size	Black and White	Slide/Movie
Location	Distance	Associated/Disassociated

The visual portion of a student's experience may be bright or dark. The size of the experience may be large, small, or somewhere in between. The location of the experience refers to where the experience is within the individual student's visual field. It could be located to the upper right, upper left, right in front of the student, down right, down left, or on either side. The experience may be in color, or black and white. Distance means that the experience may be located close to the student, or farther away. The image may be either clear or fuzzy, and it may appear as either a slide, or as a movie. When an experience is associated, the student sees it from his own eyes, he is involved in it, he is inside the experience. A disassociated experience is viewed by the student as being a separate experience, even though he may be the subject of the experience. For example, a student may mentally review an experience in which he participated, but view it as though he were seeing a movie of himself. He would be separate from both the experience and from the feelings accompanying the experience. He is an outside observer of the experience.

Auditory Submodalities

Pitch	Rhythm	Location	Volume
Tempo	Timbre	Distance	Word/Sounds
Internal/External		Association/Disassociation	

A student may have an auditory component to his visual experience, or he may have an auditory experience alone. Pitch refers to whether a sound or voice is high or low. A student may hear the timbre, the particular quality of a voice or sound. A piano and a violin can play the same note, but the sounds have different timbre. Tempo refers to the speed of a voice or sound. It may be fast, slow, or in-between. Rhythm refers to the beat, or the accent. Location refers to where the sound or voice is within the spatial field. Distance refers to whether the experience is located close to the student or far away. A sound may have a loud or soft volume. A student may hear words and/or sounds. The experience may be internal and/or external. The student may be part of the experience, (associated), or he may hear it as a detached listener, (disassociated).

---

[12]For a more complete list of submodalities, see Using Your Brain - For a CHANGE, by Richard Bandler.

Kinesthetic Submodalities

Pressure	Texture	Duration
Temperature	Movement	Location

Pressure can be applied physically to a student experiencing a kinesthetic activity, or a student can feel "pressured" because of self-produced tension. Physical temperature can be felt by students when they experience a kinesthetic activity. Texture refers to what is felt as the surface of an object is touched. Some kinesthetic experiences involve movement. Duration, or length of time, can vary in a kinesthetic event. Location refers to where in the body the experience is felt.[13]

To illustrate the importance of submodalities, and what has been stated thus far, follow these directions. Think of a pleasant experience. Think of an unpleasant experience. Using the visual submodalities list, compare the two experiences. What did you find? If your pleasant experience is smaller, farther away or dimmer, notice what happens if you make it closer, brighter and bigger. What happens if you make the unpleasant picture smaller and farther away?

Submodalities are responsible for the manner in which our brains sort and code our experience. When some of the submodalities in an intense experience are removed or altered, frequently the response to the experience is less intense. When some of the submodalities in a neutral experience are altered or added, the response can become more intense.

Try another experiment. Take an unpleasant memory and run a brief movie of the experience.... Then start at the end of the movie, be in the movie, and run it backwards in 1 1/2 seconds.... Now think of the experience again. How does it seem to you now?

Think of another unpleasant memory. Put it in movie form, and as soon as the movie starts, add a favorite march, or circus music to it. As you finish your movie, turn up the volume of the music.... Now think of the unpleasant memory. How does this memory now seem to you?

The non-verbal behavior of students will indicate when they are accessing submodalities. When students brighten a picture, the head rotates back and up. As a picture comes closer, the head moves straight back. Look for other indications of how submodalities affect sensory feedback.

The Submodality Shift

The submodality shift is a basic method for transforming one kind of experience into another. This chapter describes how to use this method with students to help them become more curious or interested, more motivated, or how to help them gain better understanding of a particular subject. The basic method, as well as specific information in the areas of understanding and motivation, was taken from Using Your Brain - For a

---

[13]Kinesthetic submodalities can also be divided according to: 1) skin senses, 2) muscle senses and internal sensations, and 3) emotions that occur as a result of evaluating other sensations and/or perceptions.

CHANGE, and is applied here to the educational context.

Building Interest/Curiosity

The submodality shift can be used in situations where a student finds himself lacking the curiosity or interest he would like to have in a particular subject. Although he does the work, he finds himself bored with it. To use the submodality shift, the teacher first has the student think of the subject he wants to be more curious about. Then the student thinks about something he is already curious about or fascinated by. The teacher identifies submodality differences between these two experiences. The teacher then tests submodalities one at a time to find out which work to make the student curious. The teacher then changes the submodalities of the "boring" experience to be like those of the "curious" experience. In this way the student's response to what had been boring, becomes that of interest or curiosity.

Scenario To Illustrate Interest/Curiosity

Jim was very interested in social studies but found it difficult to maintain an interest in math. As a result, his math grades were not as good as he wished them to be. He asked his teacher what he could do to generate an interest in math, and she told him that she thought she could help him. The submodality shift was her choice of techniques to help him.

T: "Jim, I'd like you to remember a time when you had a great deal of interest in studying your social studies."

S: "O.K. I remember a project that I found really interesting."

T: "Now, I want you to remember a time when you were really bored with math."

S: "That's not hard to remember at all!"

T: "Good. Let's compare the two pictures. Is one picture brighter than the other?"

S: Yes, the picture of the social studies project is brighter."

T: "Is one picture larger?"

S: "Yes, the social studies picture is larger."

T: "Is one picture closer?"

S: "Yes, the same picture."

T: "Is one picture clearer?"

S: "Yes, the same picture."

T: "Are there any other differences between the two pictures?"

S: "Yes. The social studies picture is like a movie, and it's in color."

T: "Excellent! Now I'd like to have you remember the math picture. Make the math picture brighter. Does that make it more interesting?"

S: "A little bit."

T: "Look at the math picture the way it used to be and now make it closer to you. Does that make it more interesting?"

S: "Yes."

T: "See the original math picture. Now make the picture clearer. Does that make it more interesting?"

S: "Somewhat."

T: "Take the old math picture and make it into a color movie. Does that make it more interesting?"

S: "Yes!"

T: "Take the old math picture, make it closer to you, and make it into a color movie. Do those changes make it interesting?"

S: "It really does!"

T: "The way for you to make math interesting is to make pictures of math that are close to you and make them look like a color movie."

The submodality shift is most apt to work if the student begins by being bored with the material. If the student has an aversive reaction, other techniques also need to be used.

Increasing Subject Matter Understanding

Knowing how a student understands material, and how he is confused about subject matter, can help the teacher ensure that learning occurs for that student. When a student has adequate information to understand the subject at hand, but has not organized it in a way that allows him to understand it, confusion occurs. If, in the teacher's opinion, a student has adequate information to understand certain subject matter, but still indicates a lack of understanding, the teacher can direct the student to think of something else within the same subject matter context that he does understand. The teacher helps the student determine the submodality differences between the two states. By determining the submodality differences, the teacher can assist the student in rearranging the data which he is confused about, into an arrangement which will lead to understanding.

Scenario To Illustrate Subject Matter Understanding

Billy has expressed some confusion about understanding how the "Electoral College" works in the election of the President. The teacher questions Billy and believes that he has enough knowledge to understand how the "College" functions, but that his organization of the information prevents him from understanding the "College's" function.

T: "Billy, you understand how the Governor is elected."

S: "Yes, I do."

T: "When you think about how the Governor is elected, and when you think about how the Electoral College works, what do you see for each?"

S: I have a picture that goes with each."

T: "I'd like to know what differences there are between the two pictures. Is one brighter than the other?"

S: "The picture about how the Governor is elected is brighter and it is bigger than the other picture."

T: "Are the pictures in color?"

S: "One is. The Electoral College picture is black and white, and the other picture is in color."

T: "Is one picture closer to you?"

S: "No, they are both close to me."

T: "Are there any other differences that you notice?"

S: "Just one. The College picture is fuzzy, and the other picture is clear."

T: (The teacher applies each submodality to the college picture as was done in the previous exercise. He finds that the big, brighter, clear and color submodalities were significant in changing the College picture.)

"Great! I'd like to have you look at the College picture. Make it bright. Make it big. Make it clear, and make it in color.

(The teacher gives Billy ample time to make those adjustments.)

"Do those changes in any way help your understanding of the College?"

S: "It makes more sense to me now. I want to reread the section in the book that explains it, and then let me tell you about it. That will be a good check to see that I really understand it."

Motivation

Most teachers are very concerned about the lack of motivation on the part of some of their students. Who hasn't heard comments in the teacher's lounge about students who never do their homework, or their projects, or don't read their assignments? Knowing how students motivate themselves, and being able to apply that information to areas where they lack motivation, is one of the best ways to change student behavior. The most common methods used by most students to motivate themselves include anxiety about what will happen if something doesn't get done, and pleasure about completing a task. Some creative students use a combination of these two motivators.

Like the previous submodality patterns, the student gives the teacher information. The teacher has the student identify something that the student wants to be motivated to do. The student then identifies something similar that he already is motivated to do. The teacher identifies the submodality differences between the two situations. By applying the submodality differences found in the situation where the student is motivated, to the situation where he is not motivated, the student can achieve motivation in the situation where it is needed. To ensure success, the student should have a clear picture of what he wants to achieve. Be sure to check the submodality of association/disassociation. This is often one of the important submodalities for motivation. For some kinds of motivation an associated picture works better; long-range motivation usually works better with a disassociated image. It is also necessary to future pace the change and to observe the sensory feedback of the student to determine the success of the change.

Scenario To Illustrate Motivation

Debra has consistently completed all of her homework assignments except for her social studies assignments. After talking with her, the teacher decided that Debra lacked the necessary motivation to do her assignments. Since Debra did want to get her social studies assignments done, he decided to use the submodality shift to help her get motivated.

T: "Debra, from what you've said, you would like to get your social studies assignments done."

S: "Yes, I just don't feel like it most of the time."

T: "What do you do regularly, even though the actual doing of it isn't fun?"

S: "I do my English assignments regularly."

T: "What do you see when you think about doing your English assignments? What do you see when you think about doing your social studies assignments?"

"What differences do you see between the two pictures? What is missing in the social studies picture that is in the English picture? For example, are both bright? Are they the same size? Are they in movie form or are they in slide form? Are you part of the pictures, or are you observing them? Are they close to you or far away? As you look at each of them do you see them in different locations?"

(In a real situation, these questions would need to be asked individually.)

S: "The English picture is brighter and larger. It is in movie form. The English picture is close to me and it is located right in front of me. The social studies picture is dim and small. It's like a picture. It has a frame around it. It's far away from me and I see it off to the left."

T: "Do you hear any sounds with either picture? Are you talking to yourself in either picture?"

S: "I can hear myself saying, 'I'll be glad to get this assignment turned in.' in the English picture. In the social studies picture I can hear myself saying, 'This would take me forever to do.'"

T: "Are there any differences between the voices?"

S: "The English voice is soft and gentle, the other voice is loud and mean."

T: (The teacher applies each submodality to the social studies picture, as was done in the previous exercise.)

"I'm going to give you some instructions. Do them as quickly as possible. I'd like to have you bring back the social studies picture. Take the frame off it, and bring it right in front of you. Make it big. Make it bright. Make it in movie form. See the picture from your own eyes. Hear the same soft and gentle voice saying, 'I'm glad to get this assignment turned in.'"

· (The teacher observes Debra's sensory feedback to be certain it matches the feedback she showed when she looked at the English picture. Satisfied that it does, he proceeds.)

"When do you want to do your social studies homework?"

S: "In the early evening when I do my other homework. I've been putting it off until the last minute, and sometimes I haven't done it at all."

T: "I want you to imagine it's next Tuesday evening, and you are about to do your social studies homework."

(The teacher watches her non-verbal behavior. He observes the desired state feedback.)

S: "It's hard to believe, but I really can imagine going right ahead with it. It seems almost as easy as to get started on my English homework."

Like all the patterns in this chapter, the results depend on performing the shift quickly. The submodality changes in the desired state picture should therefore be made rapidly.

The Swish Pattern

Richard Bandler has stated, "The Swish Pattern has a more powerful effect than any other technique I've used." Coming from Bandler, that is a profound statement. It shows how important he considers this technique.

The Swish Pattern utilizes the brain's natural ability to learn rapidly. Many of the other NLP techniques prescribe specific solutions. This unusual technique programs the brain to set a new direction without specifying exactly how to achieve it. The technique promotes generative and evolutionary change, which means that once the brain is programmed in a certain direction, positive changes result that even go beyond what the individual originally sought to change.

Although the Swish Pattern can be used with any two submodalities, (in any sensory system), the standard Swish Pattern presented below uses two visual submodalities - size and brightness - which are effective for roughly 70% of the student population.

The Standard Swish Pattern (Using Size & Brightness)

1) The student identifies the behavior or response that he wants to change and where or when he would like to have a different response.

2) The student identifies the cue picture.

   The student should identify what he sees just before he starts doing the behavior he wants to change, and he should make this into a big bright image.

   (It may help to have the student actually start to do whatever action precedes the behavior, so that the teacher may observe it. This picture should be associated; the student should see it through his eyes. The example in the following scenario will clarify this statement.)

   The sensory feedback will indicate some degree of unpleasantness.

3) The student creates an outcome picture, also big and bright.

   This is a picture of how he would see himself if he had no longer had the problem, and had more choices. This picture should be very attractive and desirable to the student. It should also be a disassociated picture, i.e. the student sees himself in the picture.

   The sensory feedback should indicate a positive and desirable image.

4) The Swish

   The student starts out by seeing the cue picture as a big, bright associated image.

   As he views the cue picture, he places a small and dim image of the outcome picture in the center of the cue picture. This small image will rapidly brighten and expand to cover the cue picture. This outcome image will stay disassociated.

   After each swish, have the student open his eyes, or blank the screen. The student should swish the pictures rapidly, (within 1½ seconds), five times.

5) Test the change.

   a) Have the student picture the first cue image. If the swish has been effective, the student will probably have difficulty seeing the image.

   b) Another way to test the change, depending upon the type of change the student is seeking, is to have the student start to do the behavior and observe his response; if the response comes from someone else's behavior, the teacher can do or say what that person does or says, and observe the student's reactions.

6) If the old behavior is still there, repeat the swish.

a) The most common reasons for the Swish not working are:

    (1)   it is performed too slowly;

          (If the student has difficulty doing the Swish in the $1\frac{1}{2}$ seconds, he may need to practice it several times or it may be helpful to chunk down the pieces. The student can practice 5 to 10 times having the cue picture become smaller and dimmer. He can then practice 5 to 10 times having the small outcome image get bigger and brighter. Finally, he can put the two together.)

    (2)   the student forgets to either blank the screen or open his eyes after each Swish;

    (3)   the image is inappropriate, or too narrowly specified;

    (4)   the outcome picture is inappropriate, because it is "unreal" - one not desirable enough.

    (5)   Size and brightness are not the most compelling submodalities for this student . In this case, you need to gather information about the most powerful submodalities and design a Swish using, for instance, "color" and "distance," instead of "size" and "brightness."

Variations of the Swish Pattern

There are many variations of the pattern set-up; below are one or two possibilities which some students may find easier to utilize. If necessary, the teacher can create Swish Pattern set-ups that will be especially appropriate for a student who has difficulty with the standard set-up.

    a)   One variation is to see the cue picture on a piece of flexible rubber with the edges held. As the cue picture is almost gone, the middle of the picture is pushed in like a tunnel, the center of the picture breaks, and the outcome image snaps back into place.

    b)   Another variation is to see the cue picture on a hinge. Above the cue picture, also attached to the hinge is the outcome image. The outcome image swings down and covers the cue picture, completing the Swish.

Scenario To Illustrate The Swish Pattern

Tim, a perceptive student, is aware that he lacks the confidence to be a better student. His teacher has been able to help him in the past to make some changes. He now asks for more assistance.

T: "Tim, I'm glad to see you again. How may I help you?"

S: "I've been thinking a lot about doing better in school. I think I could be a better student if I was more confident that I could do well."

T: "So you would like to be more confident about your ability to do well in school? That's fine."

(They discuss the advantages and disadvantages of the change.)

"Tim, I would like to have you make a picture of what you see, just before you know you aren't confident."

S: "I see my report card and it has low grades."

(This picture should be an associated one - what the student sees through his eyes.)

T: "I can see by looking at you that it was not a very pleasant experience. Describe the way the picture looks. For example, is the picture bright, big, close, etc.?

(The teacher goes through the submodalities one at a time, having Tim try each one to see which two or three create the most change in the picture and Tim's feelings. Each submodality is changed back to the way it was in the original picture before another one is examined.)

(The significant submodalities for Tim are "brightness" and "distance." He feels worse when the image is "bright" and "close.")

"Tim, if you made this change, how would you look differently? Make this picture very attractive."

(This picture should be disassociated -- the student sees himself looking extremely confident.)

S: "O.K. I have it."

(Tim's sensory feedback confirms his statement.)

T: "Tim, I'd like you to look at the first picture 'big' and 'close'. As you look at it, make a distant image of the second picture next to the first picture. The first picture is going to move away quickly and get dim. The small picture will move toward you rapidly and get brighter at the same time. As soon as you wish, open your eyes, or blank your internal visual screen.

"Do you understand? O.K., now close your eyes and make the Swish as fast as I say 'swish'. 'Swish.' Open your eyes. Do it again. 'Swish.' Open your eyes. 'Swish.'"

(The teacher continues the process for at least 5 times or until he is confident that the technique has been successful.)

"Tim, I'd like to have you look at the first picture of yourself, the one when you saw the bad report card."

S: "It's really hard to see it. It's almost gone."

There are many other "fine points" to using the Swish effectively, particularly when doing an auditory or kinesthetic swish, or a swish that uses submodalities from two different sensory systems. In addition, there are many systematic non-verbal cues that cannot be adequately described or taught in written form. As with most NLP skills, there is no substitute of supervised "hands on" exercises for thorough behavioral learning. An excellent videotape of Steve and Connirae Andreas demonstrating the standard swish and an auditory swish is available from NLP of Colorado. (See the NLP Training Section in the back of this book.)

Eliminating Strong Fears and/or Phobias

Richard Bandler has developed a disassociation technique that is excellent for eliminating abnormally strong fears or phobic responses, such as test anxiety, fear of school, fear of water, fear of insects, reactions to previous child and sexual abuse, etc. The steps are as follows:

1) The student imagines that he is sitting in a seat in the middle of a movie theatre.

2) The student makes a black and white picture or himself of how he looked just before he had the problem experience, and sees this picture on the movie theatre screen.

3) The student then allows himself to float out of his body up to the projection booth of the theatre, so that he can see himself sitting in the middle of the theatre watching the picture of himself on the screen.

4) The student turns the snapshot on the screen onto a black and white movie, and watches it from the beginning to just beyond the end of the unpleasant experience.

(For this technique to work, it is very important that the student begins and ends the movie at a safe, secure point.)

5) When the student gets to the end of the movie, he stops the movie in the last frame, jumps inside the movie and steps into himself on the screen, then runs his movie backward, in one or two seconds.

(By the term "backwards" is meant that everything is reversed -- people walk backwards, etc. Again, doing step #5 very quickly in one or two seconds, is crucial to the successful outcome to this technique. Students may wish to practice the last step several times until they are able to do it within the one to two second time frame.)

6) If possible, test the results by having the student confront the actual situation that he previously feared. If this is not possible, have the student think about the situation which previously caused him difficulty. Watch the non-verbal feedback of the student to determine the success of this technique.

Scenario To Illustrate Strong Fear/Phobia Eliminator

Jim's classroom teacher discovers that he is deathly afraid of water, and that he is very upset at the prospect of having to take swimming lessons in his physical education class. The teacher offers to help Jim, and Jim accepts.

T: "Jim, I'm gong to show you a simple way for you to eliminate your fear of water."

S: "I'd like that. I know that I will be teased by my friends, if they know that I'm afraid to get into the water."

T: "First, Jim, I'd like you to close your eyes and pretend that you're sitting by yourself in the middle of a movie theatre. When you are sitting there, nod your head.

T: "Now, I'd like you to make a picture of how you look before you get into the pool. See this picture in black and white. Nod your head when you can see this.

T: "Float out of your body and up to the projection booth of the theatre. See yourself sitting in the middle of the theatre watching yourself on the screen. Again, nod your head when you are doing that.

T: "Turn the snapshot of yourself on the screen into a black and white movie and watch it from the beginning to just beyond the end, where you are again feeling okay. Nod your head when you are finished, and keep your eyes closed.

T: "Go to the last frame of that movie, jump inside it and step into yourself in the film. Now run the movie backwards in color -- in or two seconds.

"Now, Jim, imagine yourself in your physical education class, and that you are getting ready to take swimming lessons. What is it like?"

S: "I can't believe it. I can see myself getting into the water and even putting my face into the water. I never could do that before."

T: "Jim, I'm really pleased that I could help you. Enjoy your swimming lessons."

An actual demonstration of this method eliminating a twenty-two year intense phobia of bees is available from NLP of Colordo. (See NLP Training Section in the back of this book.)

Exercise #57
Stimulating Interest/Curiosity

Purpose: To learn to stimulate interest/curiosity.

'A', 'B', and 'C' each select something they wish to be more interested in.

'B' guides 'A' through the process. 'C' coaches and then critiques 'B's work.

Rotate the roles.

Exercise #58
Increasing Subject Matter Understanding

Purpose: To learn to increase subject matter understanding.

'A', 'B', and 'C' each select some information that they are confused about and information they understand.

'B' guides 'A' through the process of increasing understanding. 'C' observes and critiques.

Rotate the roles.

Exercise #59
Increasing Motivation

Purpose: To learn to increase student motivation.

'A', 'B', and 'C' each select a context where they are motivated and a context where they are not.

'B' guides 'A' through the motivation technique. 'C' observes and critiques.

Rotate the roles.

Collateral Exercise #57

Purpose: To practice stimulating interest and curiosity.

The teacher chooses a student and assists them in making something interesting.

Collateral Exercise #58

Purpose: To help a student increase subject matter understanding.

The teacher chooses a student and helps them understand some information.

Collateral Exercise #59

Purpose: To help a student become more motivated.

The teacher selects a student who wishes to be motivated in some context, and helps them make that change.

Exercise #60
Using The Swish

Purpose: To learn to use the Swish Pattern.

'A', 'B', and 'C' each select a context where they would like to use the Swish Pattern to change their behavior.

'B' guides 'A' through the Swish. 'C' observes and critiques.

Rotate the roles.

Collateral Exercise #60

Purpose: To help a student use the Swish Pattern to achieve an outcome.

The teacher chooses a student and helps him achieve his outcome by using the Swish.

Exercise #61
Using the Strong Fear/
Phobia Eliminator

Purpose: To learn how to use this technique.

'A', 'B', and 'C' each select a strong fear or phobia that they would like to eliminate.

'B' guides 'A' through the technique. 'C' observes and critiques.

Collateral Exercise #61

Purpose: To help a student eliminate strong fear or phobia.

The teacher selects a student who would like to eliminate a strong fear and, using the technique, eliminates the fear.

Summary

Submodalities refer to the smaller components of our sensory systems. Visual submodalities may include brightness, size, color, black and white, placement, distance, clarity, a still picture or movie, and association or disassociation. Auditory submodalities may include pitch, rhythm, tempo, location, and volume. Kinesthetic submodalities may include pressure, temperature, texture, movement, duration, and location. Using the Submodality Shift in such areas as building curiosity/interest, and increasing motivation manipulates the submodalities to take advantage of the brain's natural ability to learn quickly, so that rapid and lasting behavioral change occurs. The Swish and the Strong Fear/Phobia Eliminator also bring about rapid and lasting behavioral change.

The submodality patterns briefly described in this chapter are indications of the exciting and continual developments in Neuro-Linguistic Programming. As more is learned about how the brain functions, additional techniques are being developed and others further refined. More information about these, and other submodality methods such as Changing Beliefs, is available in Using Your Brain - For a CHANGE.

Chapter 22

TYPICAL INTERVENTIONS AND THEIR RESULTS

In conjunction with several classes in which I taught teachers the techniques in this book, a follow-up assignment to use an intervention technique (either Remedial or Developmental), with a student or an adult, was given. The following examples are drawn from those assignments and are stated in the writer's words. Only names have been changed to respect privacy. The examples illustrate the rapid changes that occur through the use of the techniques and they are reasonably typical teacher responses for this assignment.

Example #1: "The person with whom I helped develop an outcome was Eric, a boy who helps my husband do chores on our farm. I had Eric as a student in my biology class this past year. It didn't take long to realize that Eric had real problems spelling and reading. Eric would never take notes in my class because he was unable to read his own writing due to both poor spelling and poor penmanship. Unfinished written assignments with misspelled words were frequently the case. Eric is very active in all sports and has recently developed an interest in weightlifting. He loves to project a 'tough guy' image and very frequently brags about how many fights he's won with some of the local boys.

"Eric came in after chores one evening and after visiting for a while we got on the topic of the course that I had just completed. I told him that I could help him with his spelling without him having to put forth too much work. He liked the idea of little work and so we started our work. It was not necessary to build rapport with Eric because I see Eric daily. I proceeded with asking a few questions for eye movement calibration and I found that he is a normally-oriented right-handed person with the exception that his visual recall seemed to occur in the position of a normal person's auditory recall. Eric's desired outcome was to become a better speller so I chose to use a Developmental Technique, the spelling learning pattern. Eric bought his first car this summer and I asked him to describe how he made the decision to buy that particular car. Eric's pattern for learning exhibited strong use of auditory internal dialogue and visual external. More visual assessing would have to be developed in his learning pattern and I proceeded by using the pattern for recalling spelling words given in the text. I guided him through the pattern using the word 'stomach.' Eric had success spelling stomach throughout the entire process of this learning pattern. Feeling very good about his achievement he decided to try another word, so we chose the word 'receive.' Eric failed to spell 'receive' correctly when he copied it down after seeing it in his visual recall position the first time. He did not have any further problems going through the rest of the pattern and he was becoming increasingly pleased with himself. I really praised his efforts and with this new confidence that was starting to build within him we continued with several more words achieving great success. Eric went home that evening and had his two brothers write down some words they thought would give him trouble and then they sealed them in an envelope which he brought with him the next afternoon. Eric had success with all of these words, with the exception of the word 'conscience.' This experience was such a positive one for both Eric and me that I've fast become a 'true believer' in the techniques!"

210

Example #2:   For my intervention plan, I chose my husband as my subject. The desired outcome which he wished to achieve was to be able to play golf with me calmly and to be able to enjoy the round. (My husband is a very good golfer and wants to teach me to be better. This causes friction and frustration as I don't take criticism well from him and as a result he gets upset. The solution was for him to hold his comments and at the same time feel calm.)

"To proceed with the intervention plan I used the following steps:

1. Calibrated Harold's eye movements and found him to be a normally-organized right-handed person.

2. Had Harold state his outcome in a positive manner.

3. Went through the evidence, context and environmental questions concerning the outcome.

4. I determined that a Remedial Technique was appropriate since this was a response which was limited to a single situation and called for a single change.

5. Because I felt the Combining Links technique was not strong enough, I used the Integrating Links technique.

   a. I asked Harold to imagine he was playing golf with me, took him through the sensory map and linked this with a visual link (a gesture).

   b. State break was established - next he chose the following resources which would help him overcome his frustration and reach his desired outcome: determination, love, joy, peace, concentration, and calmness.

   c. Each of the positive resources were linked with a kinesthetic link as he went through a sensory map for each.

   d. I tested both the negative state and the positive state and found them to be working.

   e. I integrated the negative and positive states by activating both links simultaneously.

   f. I then asked Harold to future pace. He was asked to imagine himself playing golf with me. He confided that he felt calm.

   g. The next evening we tested the effectiveness of the technique by playing golf together. Except for one time when he thought I was aiming straight at a tree and might get hurt if the ball came straight back to me, he did not offer advice or get frustrated. For my part I enjoyed the round and even scored lower than I had the last time I had played with him.

211

h. A further test of the technique came three days later. Again Harold remained calm and again I felt comfortable. This time I had the lowest score I'd ever had while playing with him!"

Example #3: "My planned intervention was with my nine year old son. He is small for his age, but has a very good sense of humor and is talkative and intelligent. He has been self-conscious about being so small. The more we talked I could tell that he wanted to have more self confidence. We sat down one afternoon and started talking. I decided to use a Remedial Technique on him. I had him focus on a time when he was feeling confident and linked it. I then focused on a time when he wasn't so confident and I linked that state. Then I integrated the two links. When we finished working together that afternoon, he told me he didn't feel so small anymore. I can tell that it helped him because he is taking swimming lessons and has really improved since our work together, even to the point of jumping off the diving board which he lacked the confidence earlier to do. It was a rewarding experience for me as well as for my son. I feel we are communicating much better and I see my son in a different light!"

Example #4: "Marcia is my niece. She is the youngest child of my oldest sister. She was born long after her brother and two sisters. She is a real joy. Marcia came to visit me, the day after class ended, for four days while her mother was out of town. The first three days went along fine. Then, her oldest sister called on Monday night. Almost immediately, I could see Marcia begin to miss the rest of the family. This presented a perfect situation for me to use a technique. I decided the Thirty-Second Link was in order. Away to the bathroom I went to review the technique. When I returned, Marcia looked close to tears. I sat down beside her and said, 'Marcia, you look sad.' Marcia replied that she was missing her Mom. I asked how she would like to feel and she responded with, 'Not so lonesome.' Then I asked if she meant by that, that she would like to feel happy and funny. Her answer was affirmative. I followed the complete technique with extra stress on remembering what she smelled and tasted, as Marcia likes to go out to eat and often does. There was definitely a change in posture in this little girl and I can see from this one instance just how important this technique will be to me this year. Being able to change Marcia's state was a very important lesson in that I, too, can do it!"

Example #5: "My client is my husband who is a 40 year-old male elementary school principal. He was an elementary physical education instructor and junior/senior high school coach in football, basketball, wrestling, and tennis for 16 years.

"Nature of the Problem: Typical Situation: If client was considering having a faculty meeting the following day, the memo needed to be typed by 3 o'clock, client 'stews' around considering whether or not the teachers would be better served by presenting the material at a teacher's meeting or in written memo form. Problem only occurs where action or decision could affect others negatively; i.e., teacher's meeting is an imposition on teacher's time if it could have been handled as effectively with a memo.

"Outcome: I would like to change stewing time to productive time.

"Decision Point: A Remedial Technique was chosen because the response calls for a single change in a single context. Response was not of long standing. Integrating Links was chosen because it is appropriate for remedial problems and I had observed and practiced it in class in order to be able to use it correctly.

"Outcome was stated in positive terms.

Evidence Questions:
(1) Increased output
(2) Pride increased
(3) Confidence increased
(4) Absence of tenseness
  in stomach and head
(5) Other's people's awareness of
  increased productivity and
  of increased patience and
  outgoingness because of not
  being wrapped up in problem

Environmental Questions:
Advantages:
(1) Better job efficiency
(2) Personally feel better about
  self & physically less tense
  & more relaxed
(3) Other person's perception
  improved

Disadvantages:
(1) Temporary easiness in
  procrastinating is gone
(2) could produce more pressure

Content Questions:
(1) With whom: wife & faculty
(2) Where: home and school
(3) When: Now.

Resources:
(1) confidence
(2) compassion & caring
(3) feeling of being healthy
(4) pride.

"Results: Both client and I considered the intervention a success. Client immediately gave personal phone calls to 9 of 11 interview job applicants to tell them that they did NOT get the job! No easy task! But confident that it is better for them that they hear personally from him about the job outcome as soon as possible."

Example #6:   "Sarah, my five year old daughter, was my client. She has always gone to her own bed to sleep at night until she was sick this past spring. Since then she sometimes doesn't feel good at bedtime and will want to sleep either in our bed or have me sleep in her bed. (Author's note: child had serious health problems and was beginnning to slowly recuperate.)

All of our family had gone to bed when Sarah called for me to come to her room. She said she didn't feel good, her stomach hurt and she wanted to come to my bed. I decided to use the Thirty-Second Integrating Link Technique, because I thought it would be the easiest and quickest for Sarah as she was getting into a negative state very quickly. I asked her how she would like to be feeling and she said she'd like to 'feel good and not hurt all over.' I finished the Thirty-Second Link and considered the outcome a tremendous success because she ended in a positive state and went to sleep in her own bed. The best part was the fact that she stayed in her own bed all night and has continued to do so since then!"

Example #7:   "My husband, Brian, was my subject. He's a 36 year old college graduate who's presently employed as a school teacher and coach. He's been serving in that capacity for the past 10 years. Brian has found that teaching is not as challenging or satisfying as it used to be and has been looking at other job possibilities. He has been offered several job opportunities the past four years but has always declined because I suspect, deep down he was basically too afraid. He's recently been made aware of a job in a field that offers excellent advancement opportunities, as well as many other benefits. He's also been advised that in all probability the job is his if he wants it. Brian submitted his application a week before class and since then has been going through a tough time deciding to take the job should it be offered, if it's the right decision for our family, if he's suited to it, etc. As much as he wants a job change, he's reluctant to make the decision to go ahead and accept.

"As I talked about things that happened in class, he jokingly suggested that maybe through what I've learned I could help him make a decision about this job. I agreed. Brian's outcome was to have confidence in making this job decision. The resources he decided he would need are: confidence, decisiveness, strength, flexibility, faith and acceptance. I decided to use a Remedial Technique because his outcome is needed in one specific situation. I decided to try the Integrating Link Technique.

"First I had Brian restate his positive outcome. Then I asked him to describe now how he feels about making this job decision. His response was 'not confident, confused, and troubled.' He labeled his present state as 'troubled.' Then I had Brian access the present state as I went through the sensory map and linked the negative state. While doing this I patted my hand on my leg. After a state break, I had Brian list his resources again. Next, I asked him to recall a time when he felt really confident. I went through the sensory mapping procedure and linked the experience by squeezing his shoulder. I followed this same procedure as I proceeded through the other 5 resources Brian listed, linking each as I went through the sensory map. After another short state break, I tested both the present state and the desired state. They were both functioning. Again I broke state and then activated both links at once. By observing Brian's sensory cues I could tell the integration process had occurred and I broke off the present state and continued linking the desired state. I told Brian, as I did this, that I knew he felt confident and 'wasn't that a good feeling' and that he would now be confident that whatever choice he made concerning this job, it would be the right one. After another short state break, I had Brian future pace. When I asked how he felt, he replied that he felt very positive, confident and assured that the job was right for him and our family and that he would take the job if it were offered.

"My on the spot decision was to have him do a K link on himself as an extra precaution. He did one for calmness and relaxation. He later said he employed that link before a recent interview concerning the job and that it worked for him.

"As I was typing up this paper, my husband was notified that he did indeed get the job pending the outcome of a physical this coming

214

weekend. We have no reason to suspect he would not pass one. Brian remains very confident that all is well with this job and he has accepted the idea. Also, since the integration process he's been so much more relaxed and good natured at home, especially with the kids."

Example #8: "I chose to do the intervention on my son Chad, who is six years old and just out of first grade. Chad had quite a problem learning his addition and subtraction facts this school year. He used his fingers to count and needs to overcome this habit as I know they will be giving him timed math tests in second grade. He must know these facts! The positive outcome was that he will be able to learn his facts without having to rely on his fingers. He agreed that it would be more fun to know the facts in his mind.

"Upon calibrating his eye movements, I discovered that he is a normally organized right-handed person. From there I decided to use a Developmental Technique and attempt to install a specific learning pattern. I used the math learning pattern suggested in the text. Chad chose blue as his favorite color. I did have quite a time getting him to 'see' his math fact in his favorite color. Thinking that perhaps it would help to install it in his world, I tried having him picture it on the 'General Lee' car, but that didn't work. He finally got the idea, though! We then proceeded with the rest of the steps. (I also used some linking by squeezing his arm and saying 'Great!' after he completed each step correctly.)

"I did not actually think that Chad would enjoy sitting down and working on math facts. However, after going through this process once, he readily agreed to try several more math facts in the same way. At long last I have found a wonderful way to help him learn his math without a bundle of tears!

"We then tried working the problems. He got them all right! I definitely feel that we did achieve Chad's positive outcome. We did do some follow-up sessions. I discovered that the more we went through the process, the easier it became for me to do the installing. Chad thought it was great fun and he is a kid who said all through the school year how much he didn't like math.

"If I were to do this all over again, I think that I would have planned out better how to explain to this six-year-old how to picture things in his favorite color. Other than that, I was quite satisfied at how this technique worked. Amazing, isn't it?"

Summary

With but one week's training in the "master teaching techniques", these teachers were able to help their clients formulate well-developed outcomes and then to select and execute techniques that altered their client's behavior. It is evident from these examples that both the teachers and their clients were all pleased: the teachers with their new-found skills and the clients with their new-found successes! My compliments to the teachers for having faith in themselves and in their new-found skills!

Chapter 23

CHOOSING AN INTERVENTION TECHNIQUE

This chapter contains several examples of situations that typically might arise during the course of the school year. Using the information that is provided for each example, determine what technique(s) you would utilize.

Example #1:   Johnny has been in your elementary classroom three months. His moods have shifted from being withdrawn to acting aggressively toward other children. Approximately a month ago it was discovered that his father was abusing Johnny and other family members. Johnny has since been removed from that environment. His aggressive behavior has ceased, but he still appears withdrawn. Assuming that he wished to feel differently, what technique would seem to be most appropriate to use to help Johnny?

Example #2:   Jane, a normally vivacious young girl, is looking depressed and sad. You decide to give her an option of feeling differently. Which technique would you use?

Example #3:   Sue is a conscientious student and highly motivated, but despite her best efforts, she does not score well on her spelling tests. How could you help her?

Example #4:   Jody is a high school sophomore in your home room. She has "attached" herself to you and she believes that you are her friend. Recently she has confided to you that she would like to be involved in more activities, have more friends, etc., but she feels she won't do well, and that she will be rejected by her classmates. You offer to help her. What will you do?

Example #5:   Melissa is trying to make up her mind about what type of high school program she should follow. She is wavering between a college-bound program and a non-college bound program. Melissa seeks your assistance. How can you help her?

Example #6:   Ben is an eighth grade student with whom you have good rapport. One day when you are talking to him, you make a comment about the fact that you can't understand why he doesn't earn better grades than he does. Ben says that he wants to do better, but something just seems to stop him from getting higher grades. He comments that it has been that way for him since the second grade. He takes you up on your offer to help him. What will you do?

Answer For Example #1:   Carefully determine Johnny's feelings and help him establish a well-formed outcome. If he desires it, and you believe it to be in his best interests, the Disassociation Technique would help him distance himself from his feelings associated with his father's abusive behavior.

Answer For Example #2:   Assuming that the situation was not a major crisis, probably the most effective technique to use would be the 30 Second Integrating Links Technique.

Answer For Example #3:   It is necessary to determine whether Sue has some emotional blockages associated with her problem or, if her visual recall pattern needs development. Help her determine a positive outcome. Emotional blockages could be altered through Integrating Links. If her visual recall needs development, she should be taught the spelling learning pattern.

Answer For Example #4:   You diagnose her problem as a poor self-concept, and help her construct a well-formed outcome. The Integrating Links technique would be a very appropriate choice. Another choice, depending upon the history of the situation, would be Revising Life Patterns.

Answer For Example #5:   You talk with Melissa about her thoughts and feelings and what she feels will be her future interests. Since Melissa has the ability to do college work and you feel this is what she really would like to do, you utilize the Two-Handed Link technique.

Answer For Example #6:   If Ben shows signs of secondary gain in his under-achievement, then the Transforming Technique would be appropriate. If there is no appearance of secondary gain, then Revising Life Patterns would be appropriate in dealing with his outcome. Also metaphors could be used to deal with the situation.

Summary

Now that you have compared your solutions to the answers that have been given, how did you fare? It is perfectly acceptable if your answers differ from the answers given, provided you have good reasons for your choice.

If you were to select a technique and for some reason it didn't work, remember to redo the technique (particularly if it was not well done the first time), or to try another technique. Flexibility will help to ensure success!

Chapter 24

ODDS N' ENDS

What are further practical applications for Master Teaching Techniques?

Counselors

Counselors are in a unique position. They often have more flexibility regarding time and the possibility of having a one-to-one relationship with students than do most classroom teachers. These <u>Master Teaching Techniques</u> allow counselors to better achieve their goals and to assist students in dealing more creatively and effectively with life's complexities. Counselors can also help train teachers in the use of these techniques.

Parent-Teacher Conferences

Parent-teacher conferences can be a delightful or a horrendous experience depending upon the reason for the conference, the human relations skills the teacher possesses and the attitude of the parent(s). Building rapport through pacing and leading should be a goal for every teacher. Using change state techniques may be very helpful in altering parental moods. The use of visual and auditory links may be appropriate in achieving certain responses. A Visual Scramble linking technique could prove helpful in dealing with certain situations. For example, let us suppose that the teacher believes the parent needs to institute certain measures that would be helpful to the child. To ensure parental cooperation the teacher, as the meeting is summed up, could extend either the right or left hand to that side of his body. Keeping the hand clearly visible and looking at it, the teacher describes the present state situation and the fact that previous efforts to resolve the situation have been unsuccessful. Then, still holding that hand out, the teacher extends the other hand out opposite the first hand, focuses attention on that hand, and describes the new techniques that will help to resolve the problem. Different voice tones should be used with each link. Then, still using the voice tone that is allied with the solutions and saying something like, "Won't it be nice not to have to deal with this situation any more?", the teacher employs a Visual Scramble by bringing both hands together and integrating the fingers of both hands. There may be a look of momentary confusion on the face of the parent as the integration of the new solutions and the old responses occur. If momentary confusion occurs, use this time to make statements, which act as commands. For example, "You will now be able to do ____ and ____ and it will help _____ (the student)." Then, stress the fact that the situation is now being resolved. The Visual Scramble is a very effective Integrating Link technique which can be used in a variety of situations, including those when touching a student proves to be difficult.

Alleviating Stress and Tension

Teacher stress and tension can be reduced by applying <u>Master Teaching Techniques</u> to the classroom. Be particularly aware that your internal state and physiology are matched and that your internal state can be changed by altering your physiology. Therefore, "stuck" states can be changed by using any state change technique. Establishing your own link to produce calmness and tranquility may be beneficial. Also, developing one or more "States of Excellence" through the exercise described in Chapter 16 can be an excellent way to alleviate stress and tension.

Personal and Professional Development

Master Teaching Techniques contains powerful tools for both personal and for professional development! While it is possible to use change of state exercises, outcome identification, and some of the simple linking techniques on your own, it may be necessary to receive some assistance from another person with training before the more complicated Remedial and Developmental techniques can be fully utilized.

It is advantageous to form a study group and to do the training exercises. The study group members can actually become resource personnel to provide assistance for each other in promoting personal and/or professional change.

Using the Skills and Feeling Comfortable with Them

Sometimes when teachers first realize the power of these techniques, there is a fear and a reluctance on their part to use them with students because parents will "find out," or the students may be adversely affected, or the principal won't approve, or the skills are too manipulative. These feelings are understandable and the underlying message may be that, "I'm not comfortable yet with the techniques." There are various ways of handling these feelings. One way is to continue functioning as in the past. Another way is to realize that you are paid to influence students, and that many teachers are already intuitively using the techniques. Then, would it not be wise and advantageous to refine your skill in using the techniques and to consciously integrate them to improve your teaching effectiveness? Skillful teachers will find that with practice it may not be necessary to follow the formalized steps of some of the techniques, but that the outcome can be achieved in creative ways using the basic techniques. An example would be using the 30 Second Integrating Link Technique rather than the formal Integrating Link technique.

Anything can be accomplished in education if one's needs are strong enough and one is creative. There is only one note of caution: First try the techniques in a non-critical situation! This practice will ensure your successful use of the techniques in a critical situation. Also, since these techniques are powerful, use them with respect and in a loving manner!

Teaching Students Master Teaching Techniques

Perhaps the most significant suggestion is this last one: Teach Students The Skills So That They Can Better Learn Material!

My wish for you is contained in this metaphor:

Once upon a time a lonely caterpillar looked longingly toward the sky. Oh, how he wanted to fly, just like the beautiful butterflies that he saw lazily floating in the big blue sky! One day, a butterfly flew close to him, and the caterpillar wistfully called out, "Butterfly, oh butterfly, when will I fly?" The butterfly smiled a warm, loving smile and replied, "Soon, little caterpillar, very soon." The caterpillar was very disappointed. His longing continued. The next day another butterfly flew close to him and the caterpillar called out again, "Butterfly, oh butterfly, when will I fly?" The butterfly lovingly replied, "Soon, little caterpillar, soon." Dismayed, the caterpillar tried to forget his dream of flying, but he could not. Soon he experienced internal changes that momentarily interrupted his dream. As the comforting folds of a chrysalis wrapped around him giving him a feeling of security, his dream of flying intensified. Much to his amazement, he emerged from the chrysalis, at the appropriate time, as a beautiful butterfly. His dream of being able to fly was at last realized! He spread his wings and launched himself into the sky. How good it felt to fly! As he soared over the meadow, he heard the plaintive voice of a caterpillar calling up to him saying, "Butterfly, oh butterfly, when will I fly?" And the butterfly looked down at the caterpillar, smiled a loving smile, and warmly replied, "Soon, little caterpillar, soon."

APPENDIX

Chapter Two

Practice Activity A: pp. 31-32.

In most instances these answers will be appropriate for each type of teacher. It would probably be difficult to find one teacher who totally fits a V, A or K mold.

A	lecture used
K	role playing emphasized
A	student talk encouraged
V	bulletin boards decorated
V	filmstrips and movies shown
A	audio tapes played
K	activities requiring manipulation utilized
V	materials neatly organized
V&K	written work stressed

A	reading aloud expected
K	student-made projects and models assigned
V	posters and signs displayed
V&K	chalkboard heavily used
A&V	math flashcards - examples and answer read aloud
V	daily work schedule listed on board
V	desks face teacher
K	learning aids 3-dimensional and manipulative

Chapter 3

Practice Activity B: p. 41

V	glimpse of the future
US	a true belief
O	sweet on it
K	grasp it
A	loud mouth
K	feel changed
V	colorful ideas
A	quiet person
US	think smart
US	learn quickly

A	harmonize here
K	was pressured
A	in tune
O	yummy solution
V	in focus
O	stale news
A	modulated voice
K	oily situation
K	ticklish situation
V	correct perspective

The sentences created for the Matching Response and for the Translation Answers are examples of the way that such sentences are written. They are not to be considered THE correct answers.

1. "People usually see me as I see myself."
   S.S.U.:   V
   M.R.:   "I see myself as I am."
   T: "I hear comments about myself that I agree with." (A)
                    "The feelings that people have toward me are the same that I have about myself." (K)

2. "I need to get in touch with my joy."
   S.S.U.:   K
   M.R.:   "I would like to feel my joy."
   T.:   "I would like to visualize myself expressing my joy." (V)
                    "I would like to hear my sounds of joy." (A)

3. "I get many fresh ideas."
   S.S.U.:   O
   M.R.:   "I get many sweet thoughts." (O)
   T.:   "I get many sharp ideas." (K)
                    "I get many clear impressions." (V)

4. "Things are beginning to click."
   S.S.U.:   A
   M.R.:   "Things are beginning to sound in harmony."
   T.:   "Things are beginning to loosen up and fall into place." (K)
                    "Things are beginning to seem in focus." (V)

5. "This is the real bright spot in my life."
   S.S.U.:   V
   M.R.:   "That situation brings sunshine into my life."
   T.:   "That situation amplifies the good things in my life." (A)
                    "That's one of the smooth situations in my life." (K)

6. "I feel close ties to my family."
   S.S.U.:   K
   M.R.:   "I feel a firm connection with my family."
   T.:   "There is harmony in the relationship between my family and me." (A)
                    "It is clear to the observer that my family and I have a good relationship." (V)

1. Answers are from left to right, matching the pictures:

   $K \quad A_d^i \quad A^c \quad V^c \quad A^r$

2. Again, answers are from left to right.

   $K \quad V^c \quad A^r \quad A_d^i \quad A^c$

   (If you found it easier to determine eye movement patterns when correlating them to predicate usage, you have just "chunked up.")

3. Answers are from left to right. The eye movement patterns would match the following symbols. (This assumes a normally-organized right-handed person.)

   $A^r \quad A_d^i \quad V^c \quad V^r \quad K$

4. Answers are from left to right. Remember to go with the eye movement patterns when determining your answer.

   $K \quad V^c \quad A_d^i \quad V^r \quad A_d^i$

Outcome Questions

1. What do you want? (stated positively)

2. How would you know you achieved it? (emphasize sensory feedback)

3. In what context do you want it?

4. What are the advantages in changing?

5. What are the disadvantages in changing?

Simplified Integrating Links Steps

1. Identify the present state.

2. Visually and auditorily link the present state using the sensory map:

   V^e — Remember what you saw at the time.

   V^i — Recall any internal images you experienced at the time.

   A^e — Recall any sounds, voices or noises you heard.

   A^i — Remember any internal dialogue there may have been.

   K^e — If there were any external feelings, recall them.

   K^i — Remember your internal feelings.

   O^e — Recall any smells or tastes associated with this experience.

   O^i — If any remembered smells or tastes were triggered by this experience, recall them.

3. Break state.

4. Have students identify needed personal resources.

persistence	tenderness
anger	caring
confidence	love
strength	inflexibility
flexibility	organization
happiness	adventurousness
joy	decisiveness
stubbornness	helpfulness
compassion	humor
disassociation	cleverness

5. Kinesthetically and auditorily link the desired state using the sensory map.

6. Break state.

7. Test each link with a state break in between.

8. Integrate both links, using positive comments made in the desired state auditory tonality.

9. Break state.

10. Future pace.

Using Integrating Links for Self-Help

1.   Identify your present state.

2.   Kinesthetically link your present state using the sensory map.

3.   Break state.

4.   Select the necessary personal resources that you need.

persistence	tenderness
anger	caring
confidence	love
strength	inflexibility
flexibility	organization
happiness	adventurousness
joy	decisiveness
stubbornness	helpfulness
compassion	humor
disassociation	cleverness

5.   Use a different K link to link the desired state.

      (Be certain this is a very powerful link.)

6.   Break state.

7.   Test each link.

8.   Integrate both links.

9.   Break state.

10.   Future pace.

Simplified Revising Life Patterns Steps

1. Help the student determine a positive outcome.

2. K link the negative state response.

3. Direct the student to drift back in time remembering other times when he had the same response, and have him remember the first time the response occurred.

   (The student can nod his head each time he remembers such an instance.)

4. Use the same K link and lightly tap the link each time the student remembers an instance.

5. Establish a positive K link, (one way is to hold the student's hand), and ask: "If you knew then what you know now, what additional choices or resources could you have used?"

   a) Squeeze the hand each time a choice or resource is mentioned.

6. Continue holding the hand link and ask the student to make a picture of that younger person that was him.

   a) Ask the student to tell the younger person what would have been helpful for him to know so that he could have felt and/or acted differently.

7. Direct the student to return to the earliest negative experience that he can remember.

8. Have the student nod his head as he remembers each experience from the earliest instance to the most recent.

9. Each time he nods his head, integrate the links by squeezing the hand link while lightly tapping the negative link.

10. Future pace.

Simplified Disassociation Steps

1. Help the student determine a positive outcome.

2. Direct the student to select a disassociated situation.   Link it kinesthetically.

3. Ask the student to recall his "stuck state" situation.

4. Activate the K link and "pop" the student out of the "stuck state."

5. Have the student select resources that would help him achieve his outcome.

6. Using the same K link that was used in Step 2, link each resource.

7. Direct the student to recall the "stuck state."

8. Activate the link and hold until the disassociation is complete.

9. Observe the sensory feedback to determine the technique's success.

Simplified Transforming Steps

1. Direct students to identify and state, in positive form, the behavior they want changed.

2. Label the part.

3. Establish communication with the part.

4. Direct students to find out the intent of the part.

5. Have students thank the part for its behavior.

6. Instruct students to contact their creative part for <u>at least</u> 3 new choices that will satisfy the intention of the original part.

   (High-quality and realistic responses are necessary for the success of this technique.)

   ## AND/OR

   Talk directly to the creative part and instruct it to create alternatives which will meet the needs of the other part.

   "I want to speak directly to your creative part and to instruct it to create alternatives which will meet the needs of ___. You will probably not be aware of these new alternatives because they will come to you unconsciously. They may come to you <u>immediately,</u> they may come to you as you dream tonight, they most certainly will come to you within the next few days, (or they will come as soon as you are ready for them). You will know that they have come because your behavior will have changed."

7. Have students ask the original part if it has any objection to the new choices.

8. Instruct students to ask if any other parts have any objection to the new choices.

   (Should there be any objections in either Step 7 or Step 8, return to Step 6 and have the creative part generate more choices. Check again for any objections before proceeding to Step 9.)

9. Future pace.

10. Thank the parts.

Using Transforming for Self-Help

1. Identify and state in a positive form the behavior you want changed.

2. Label the part.

3. Establish communication with the part.

4. Thank the part for its behavior.

5. Establish the intent of the part.

6. Contact your creative part for <u>a minimum</u> of 3 new choices to satisfy the intention of the original part.

    (Selecting realistic and high quality choices is essential!)

7. Recontact the original part and get its acceptance of the new choices and its promise to implement them.

8. Determine if any other parts object to the new choices.

9. Future pace.

10. Thank the parts.

ABOUT THE AUTHOR

Bernard F. Cleveland has taught at all levels of the public school: elementary, junior high, and high school. Dr. Cleveland has also taught elementary and secondary methods courses and he has supervised elementary and secondary student teachers. In addition, he has taught many graduate in-service courses for teachers in several states. His Ph.D. was earned at the Ohio State University.

Dr. Cleveland is an educational, athletic, and business consultant. Through his company, The Connecting Link, he teaches and uses powerful tools and techniques that link people with their resources so that they may better fulfill their potential and consistently maintain states of excellence! Master Teaching Techniques is his second book.

NLP TRAINING

The next several pages list some of the organizations and people who are involved in NLP training.

Bernard F. Cleveland, Ph.D
The Connecting Link SM
P.O. Box 716
Stone Mountain, GA 30086
(404) 979-8013

Dr. Cleveland has literally trained hundreds of business leaders, salespeople, teachers, and coaches the NLP techniques. His corporate client is Texas Utilities Company.

Dr. Cleveland offers a variety of seminars that are tailored to the needs of his clients. He is available for:

Education Inservices

Teacher Training

Coaches Training

Sales Training

Management Training

Dr. Cleveland also works with individual athletes and/or athletic teams to improve their performance.

Comprehensive NLP Training

NLP of Colorado, co-directed by Steve and Connirae Andreas, provides thorough, in-depth NLP training at all levels of Certification: Practitioner, Master Practitioner, Advanced Submodalities, and Trainer. Certification trainings are available in many Western states, and in some metropolitan areas, nationally and internationally. Residential trainings are available for those living elsewhere. Introductions to NLP, Phobia/Trauma seminars, business and sales, and other specialty seminars are also offered.

NLP OF COLORADO
1221 Left Hand Canyon Dr. JSR
Boulder, CO 80302
(303) 442-1102

NLP TRAINING VIDEOTAPES

JOHN GRINDER

These videotapes were edited from the last 4 days of a 24-day NLP Practitioner Training in Boulder, Colorado, in June 1985, and they presuppose knowledge of the basic NLP patterns. John demonstrates, talks, answers questions, tells stories, and conducts exercises to integrate knowledge, both consciously and unconsciously. These tapes will be useful not only for those who want to learn what John is teaching, but also those who would like to model how John teaches so exquisitely.

1. Human Excellence: John teaches how to elicit, anchor, and utilize accelerated learning states through metaphors, exercises, and tasking. This tape is an excellent example of John's teaching style, simultaneously directed at participants' conscious and unconscious minds. 107 minutes, $85.

2. Perceptual Styles and Masks: This tape begins with the "masks" exercise in which the behavioral impacts of different perceptual filters is explored. John goes on to delineate the different classes of NLP interventions and alternate styles of working with ecology. 114 minutes, $85.

3. Context-free Consulting: Starting with a non-verbal covert shaping exercise, John moves on to content-free consulting, in which the negotiator asks the client to carry out certain processes without knowing much about the content. Metaphoric ways of achieving the same outcome are also demonstrated and discussed. 100 minutes, $85.

All three tapes $215 (this is a 15% reduction).

CONNIRAE AND STEVE ANDREAS

These videotapes of NLP Training sessions and/or NLP work with individuals were created and produced by Connirae and Steve Andreas.

1. The Fast Phobia/Trauma Cure. An intense 20-year phobia of bees is eliminated in 6 minutes, using the fast phobia/trauma cure developed by Richard Bandler. An introduction and discussion accompanies the session, and includes an 11-month follow-up interview with the client. Also included is a 15-minute follow-up interview with a Vietnam Veteran whose "post-traumatic stress syndrome" lasting 12 years was completely changed in one session using this method. 42 minutes, $50.

2. Changing Beliefs. The belief change pattern developed by Richard Bandler is demonstrated in an Advanced NLP Submodalities Training. An explanation of what is being done accompanies the demonstration, and is followed by questions, discussion and preparation for a practical exercise using the pattern. A three-month follow-up interview with the client is also included.

104 minutes, $85.

3. Future-Pacing: Programming Yourself to Remember Later. How people program themselves to remember something automatically in the future is explored in this session taken from the second day of a 24-day NLP Practitioner Training in January, 1985. 79 minutes, $65.

4. The Swish Pattern. An amazingly rapid and powerful new submodality intervention is first demonstrated on a simple habit, nail biting. An auditory Swish is then demonstrated with a woman who went into barely-controlled rages when her daughter spoke in a certain voice tone. The demonstration includes gathering precise information to design a Swish tailored to this client. Follow-up information for both is incuded. (71 minutes, $65)

5. Available Soon: Other Tapes in Preparation. Write for a current list.

Order from NLP of Colorado. All prices postpaid within the U.S. Specify VHS or BETA.

All these video tapes are also available in the European PAL Systems at the same prices, plus airmail shipping (1 tape, $15; 2 tapes, $25; 3 tapes, $30; 4 tapes, $35. Since 5 tapes exceed the weight limit for one package, the 5th tape costs the same as one tape, $15). Please send a check or money order drawn on a U.S. bank in U.S. dollars.

NEW LEARNING PATHWAYS™

New Learning Pathways™ has reorganized. One center, New Pathways To Learning™, is located in Denver; the other, New Learning Principles™, is centered in California. These learning centers specialize in using NLP in education. They work with students of all ages. Their learning strategies are exciting, fast, and effective.

For example, the reading program allows students to gain a minimum of one grade level in eight hours of work. They use standardized tests to score results.

Both organizations also trains educators in learning techniques. They offer inservices and intensive summer workshops, where teachers learn the same techniques they use to help students make dramatic leaps in their academic skills.

For information about learning programs, or educator inservices or training, please contact:

New Pathways to Learning

1183 S. Monaco Parkway

Denver, CO 80224

(303) 758-6361

New Learning Principles

East 1000 Oaks Blvd., #142

Thousand Oaks, CA 91362

(805) 495-4836 Ext. 2018

Glossary

Calibration. The ability to read non-verbal feedback and to associate it with an individual's internal state.

Combining Links. Combining Links occurs when several powerful experiences associated with students' resources are combined to form a powerful stimulus.

Decision Point. The time when a decision is made to choose which specific intervention technique to use.

Desired State. A physiological-psychological state indicating a person is functioning in a state of excellence. Also, a positive physiological-psychological state.

Developmental Techniques. Techniques that are used when a specific outcome is sought in more than one situation or context, or when secondary gain is present. For example, long-standing lack of motivation in a subject would fall into this category. Developmental Techniques include: Transforming, Eliciting and Installing Learning Patterns, and Using Metaphors.

Disassociation. A technique designed to prevent students from experiencing strong feelings that they wish to avoid.

Dominant Sensory System. The sensory system through which an individual most consciously processes information. Predicate patterns and eye movement patterns serve as dominant sensory system indicators.

Entry Cues. Involuntary eye movement patterns, breathing patterns, muscle tone and posture changes, vocal tonal and tempo changes, facial skin coloration, and gestures are all examples of entry cues. These cues indicate what sensory system(s) people are using to process information internally.

Future Pacing. In lieu of an actual situation, students test the success of an intervention by mentally projecting themselves into the future in a situation where they would normally experience the old response. By watching students' sensory feedback, teachers can determine the probable success of the intervention. (Students should exhibit sensory signs of the desired state.)

Integrating Links. Two states, a negative and a positive one, are separately linked and the links are then activated simultaneously. The two responses are then unconsciously integrated and the student automatically has more response options in a given situation then he previously had. (Also known as "collapsing anchors".)

Leading. Leading is a test to see if rapport has been established. The person attempting to establish rapport makes a subtle change in his behavior. If rapport has been established, the student will follow that lead and alter his behavior accordingly.

Learning Patterns. Learning patterns are formed by simple and complex arrangements of sensory systems. Such patterns allow students to develop and execute a behavior. Learning patterns can be elicited by: asking questions, and/or watching eye movement patterns as a student repeats a skill or procedure. The installation of learning patterns is a result of repetition and linking.

Glossary (Continued)

Linking. A process whereby a stimulus is used to create a highly predictable response from a student. These stimuli may be visual, auditory, kinesthetic, olfactory/gustatory, or a combination of all of them. (Also known as "anchoring".)

Metaphors. Metaphors are anecdotes, parables and stories, which if constructed and used correctly, may result in long-term behavioral change.

Mirroring. A technique of subtly matching one or more of the following: eye movement patterns, facial expressions, gestures and posture, in an effort to establish rapport.

Pacing. The process used by people to establish rapport. This process includes matching predicates and/or voice tone, volume and tempo, mirroring techniques, switching, and then leading. The purpose of pacing is to establish conscious and unconscious rapport.

Predicate Patterns. Predicates refer to the use of adjectives, verbs, adverbs and other descriptive words. Some students have a tendency to speak in terms of visual, auditory or kinesthetic predicates. By identifying such patterns, teachers can frequently tell how a student processes information. Matching predicate patterns is one way to establish rapport with a person.

Present State. An undesirable or negative physiological-psychological state in which an individual lacks the resources or knowledge to change his state to a more positive state. Also, a "stuck state."

Rapport. A state in which a person is most responsive to us.

Relevancy Challenge. A technique which keeps conversation or discussions on task.

Remedial Techniques. Techniques that are used when a specific outcome is sought in one context. For example, newly-developed lack of motivation in a subject would fall into this category. Remedial Techniques include: Linking, Combining Links, Integrating Links, Revising Life Patterns, and Disassociation.

Resources. Traits, experiences, or states that help students achieve outcomes.

Revising Life Patterns. An Integrating Links Technique that neutralizes a long-term unwanted response by helping a student go back in time to deal with the origin of the response and the subsequent times that that response has affected his life.

Secondary Gain. A gain, often on the unconscious level, that encourages students to act out unacceptable or damaging behavior. Examples could include academic underachievement, over-eating, smoking and substance abuse.

Sensory Acuity. The ability to be aware of sensory feedback.

Sensory Set. The five sensory systems (visual, auditory, kinesthetic, and olfactory/gustatory), combined.

Sensory Systems. The systems that enable us to see, hear, feel, taste and smell.

Glossary (Continued)

Single Sentence Transforming. A statement designed to change either the <u>meaning</u> attached to a desirable stimulus, or the <u>context</u> attached to that stimulus. Such statements may result in students' perspectives being changed, which may result in attitudinal and behavioral changes.

Strong Fear/Phobia Eliminator. A technique that eliminates strong fears or phobias literally in minutes.

Stuck State. An undesirable or negative physiological-psychological state.

Submodalities. The components that make up each modality or sensory unit. They enable our brains to sort and code our experience.

Submodality Patterns. A variety of patterns which incorporate and use the submodalities to bring about rapid behavioral change.

Swish Pattern. A submodality pattern that programs the brain in a specific direction.

Switching. Matching one sensory system by shifting into another. An example would be to pace a students' speech tempo (auditory representation), by moving a pencil at the same tempo (a visual representation).

Thirty-Second Integrating Link. A simplified method of Integrating Links.

Transforming. A technique that changes students' responses to an experience when that response indicates the presence of secondary gain. (Also known as "reframing".)

Two-Handed Link. A method used to influence students to make decisions that the teacher considers appropriate.

Visual Scramble. A two-handed link that can be used to integrate new ideas and behaviors.

BIBLIOGRAPHY

Bandler, Richard. Using Your Brain - For a CHANGE. Mohab, Utah: Real People Press, 1985.

Bandler, Richard, and Grinder, John. Frogs Into Princes. Utah: Real People Press, 1979.

_____. Reframing. Utah: Real People Press, 1982.

Barbe, Walter B., and Swassing, Raymond H. Teaching Through Modality Strengths. Columbus, Ohio: Zaner-Bloser, Inc., 1979.

Canfield, Jack and Wells, Harold. 100 Ways To Enhance Self-Concepts In The Classroom. New Jersey: Prentice-Hall, 1976.

Dilts, Robert, Grinder, J., Bandler, R., Bandler, L.C., and DeLozier, J. Neuro-Linguistic Programming, Vol. I. Cupertino, California: Meta Publications, 1980.

Dilts, Robert. "Neuro-Linguistic Programming in Education," A Pamphlet. Santa Cruz, California: Not Limited, LTD., 1980.

Gazzaniga, Michael S. The Social Brain. New York: Basic Books, Inc., 1985.

Grinder, Michael. The Educational Conveyor Belt. Battle Ground, Washington, 1986.

Gordon, David. Therapeutic Metaphors. California: Meta Publications, 1978.

Harper, Linda. Classroom Magic. Troy, Michigan: Twiggs Communications, 1982.

Jacobson, Sid. Meta-Cation. California: Meta Publications, 1983.

Lankton, Steve. Practical Magic. California: Meta Publications, 1980.

McCarthy, Bernice. The 4Mat System. Arlington Heights, Illinois: Excel, Inc., 1980.

Miller, George A. "The Magical Number, SEVEN, Plus or Minus Two...." The Psychological Review, 63, No. 2 (March, 1956), 81-96.

Robbins, Anthony. Unlimited Power. New York: Simon and Schuster, 1986.

Van Nagel, C., Siudzinski, Robert, Reese, Edward J., and Reese, Mary Ann. Megateaching And Learning. Indian Rock Beach, Florida: Southern Institute Press, 1985.

Adding Resources, 117-119
Analytic Learner, 62-63

Brain, 61-63
Breathing Changes, 54-55

Calibration, 87-89
Chunking, 18-19
Combining Links, 137-138
Common-Sense Learner, 62-63
Counselors, 218
Creative Writing Learning
   Pattern, 172-173

Decision Point, 125-127
Developmental Frame, 126
Developmental Techniques, 155-168
Disassociation, 146-147, 230
Dominant Sensory System, 29-32
Dynamic Learner, 62-63

Entry Cues, 49-60
Entry Cues Summary, 57
Eye Entry Cues, 52
Eye Movement Patterns, 49-54, 59-60

Facial Skin Color Changes, 56
Follow Instructions Pattern, 181-182
Future Pacing, 137

Gestures, 56

Identifying Outcomes, 95-98
Information Gathering Model, 105-109
Innovative Learner, 62-63
Integrating Links, 138-142, 227-228

Leading, 82-83
Learning Pattern Elicitation, 161-165
Learning Pattern Installation, 166-167
Learning Styles, 61-63
Learning "Wheel", x
Linking, 130-137
Linking and the Classroom, 153

Math Learning Pattern, 170-171
McCarthy, Bernice, 62-63
Metaphor Construction, 190-192
Mirroring, 82

Model of the World, 19
Motivation Learning Pattern, 173, 199-201
Negative Linking, 131
New Learning Pathways, 176-188
Outcome Questions, 96-97

Pacing, 82-84
Parent-Teacher Conferences, 218
Personal Resources List, 118
Physical Classroom Environment, ix
Positive Linking, 130-131
Posture and Muscle Tone Changes, 55
Predicate Patterns, 22, 39-43, 46
Principles of Learning, xi-xiii
Principles of Teaching, 77-79
Problem Solving Pattern, 189-190

Rapport, 81-84
Reading Comprehension Pattern, 183-185
Relevancy Challenge, 121-122
Remedial Frame, 126
Remedial Techniques, 129-148
Revising Life Patterns, 144-146, 229

Secondary Gain, 126, 156
Sensory Awareness, 22
Sensory Coding, 27-28
Sensory Map, 132
Sensory Set, 28
Sensory Systems, 27-37, 161
Single-Sentence Transforming, 157
Spelling Learning Pattern, 171-172, 184-186
State Changes, 20-21
State of Excellence Link, 132
Stress and Tension, 218
Strong Fear/Phobia Eliminator, 205-206
Submodality Patterns, 194-205
Swish Pattern, 201-205
Switching, 82

Teacher Intervention Structured
   Overview, 74
Teaching, 72
Teaching "Wheel", 73
Test Anxiety, 126, 131
Thirty Second Integrating Link, 142
Tonal and Tempo Changes, 55-56
Transforming, 156-161, 231-232
Two-Handed Link, 142

Vision Information, 178-180, 184
Visual Scramble, 143